MW00559881

For Love *of* Country

Leave the Democrat Party Behind

TULSI
GABBARD

Since 1947
REGNERY
An Imprint of Skyhorse Publishing, Inc.

Regnery books may be purchased in bulk at special discounts for sales promotion, corporate gifts, fund-raising, or educational purposes. Special editions can also be created to specifications. For details, contact the Special Sales Department, Regnery, 307 West 36th Street, 11th Floor, New York, NY 10018 or info@skyhorsepublishing.com.

Regnery® is an imprint of Skyhorse Publishing, Inc.®, a Delaware corporation.

Visit our website at www.regnery.com.
Please follow our publisher Tony Lyons on Instagram @tonylyonsisuncertain.

10 9 8 7 6 5 4 3 2 1

Library of Congress Cataloging-in-Publication Data is available on file.

Cover design and photograph by Abraham Williams

Print ISBN: 978-1-68451-485-4
eBook ISBN: 978-1-68451-497-7

Printed in the United States of America

I dedicate this book to every American who loves our country and cherishes peace and freedom.

Contents

Prologue
Sounding the Alarm

I love our country. I have committed my life to defending the safety, security, and freedom of the American people. Our country is in the midst of an existential crisis.

I have friends who are Democrats, Republicans, Independents, and Libertarians. I have nothing but respect for all of them. Some work in the field of politics, but most do not. This book is not being written out of spite or animosity toward anyone because of their political affiliation. My message to you is an urgent warning: Those in control of today's Democrat Party and permanent Washington are leading us down a very dangerous path that threatens our freedom, democracy, and ability to thrive in a peaceful, prosperous country.

Regardless of your political affiliation or leanings, or which candidate you like or dislike, we should all be alarmed when those who are driven by their insatiable hunger for power are actively undermining our democracy without care for the short- and long-term consequences of their actions. They are doing all they possibly can to keep the American people from being able to choose who we want to vote for as president. They have no respect for us and our fundamental rights as citizens in a democratic republic. They are so afraid that we, the people, might make "the wrong choice" that in the name of protecting our democracy and saving us from ourselves, they are destroying our democracy and taking away our freedom to decide who our next president should be.

To make matters worse, those leading this fight really believe they're doing the right thing. They say, with great concern in their voice, that if the American people elect Donald Trump again, he will destroy our democracy and be the dictator-in-chief. This is why they feel they are justified in trying to take away our right to vote for any candidate we choose . . . in other words, they say they need to destroy our democracy in order to "save" it.

This is lunacy. It's the mindset and mentality of dictators.

As of this writing, Colorado and Maine took unprecedented action to try to remove the leading Republican candidate for president, Donald J. Trump, from their presidential primary ballots. Similar challenges have been raised in thirty-two states. In defiance of the Constitution, these people are single-handedly attempting to take away the right of American citizens to vote for Trump for president—even though he has not been charged, indicted, or convicted of the crime of insurrection they're accusing him of. Colorado's State Supreme Court made this decision in a 4–3 vote. In Maine, the decision was made unilaterally by the secretary of state, who is not a lawyer, and is a Democrat and vocal Biden supporter, and someone who actively supported impeaching Trump when he was president. Hardly an unbiased arbiter.

The precedent has been set. What's to stop Republican secretaries of state from unilaterally deciding to take President Biden off the ballot? Nothing. Reacting to efforts to remove Trump from the ballot, Missouri secretary of state Jay Ashcroft posted on X, "What has happened in Colorado & Maine is disgraceful & undermines our republic. While I expect the Supreme Court to overturn this, if not, Secretaries of State will step in & ensure the new legal standard for @realDonaldTrump applies equally to @JoeBiden!"[1]

Those behind this are not putting all their eggs in one basket, though. This is a multi-front battle, and they will stop at nothing until they're successful. "Progressive" Congressman Ro Khanna from California, who I've known for years, so desperately wants Trump off the ballot that he is demanding that the supposedly nonpartisan chairman of the Federal Reserve intervene and take action to stop the former president from getting reelected. On December 27, 2023, Rep. Khanna said in a post on X that Federal Reserve Chair Jerome Powell "should cut interest rates now given most of inflation was caused by supply shocks. If he doesn't, he may be the person most responsible for the possible return of Trump."

The Democrat elite and their cronies are using our criminal justice system to prosecute and distract the Republican presidential candidate in the midst of a presidential campaign. As a result, Donald Trump currently faces 91 charges in four criminal cases—44 federal charges and 47 state charges, all felonies. They are hoping they'll be able to convict Donald Trump of some crime—any crime—to undermine his support and thus prevent what they fear most: a second Trump presidency.

What's at stake here is far greater than Donald Trump and Joe Biden. Our democracy is being destroyed by the permanent Washington elite in both political parties who truly believe they—and not the American people—have the right and duty to determine who we want to serve and lead our country. They readily dismiss the U.S. Constitution, the rule of law, and the voices of the American people, anointing themselves as the ones who have the power and justification to decide who will become president.

Those of us who love our great country must be deeply saddened, outraged, even frightened by this reality: elected and non-elected entities who are in control of our country have no respect for the will of the American people. None. They don't care about us. They don't care about what we want. But they are afraid of us. Just like foreign dictators are afraid of democracy, the Democrat elite are so afraid of a free society and the possibility that the American people will make "the wrong choice" in this election (by choosing someone other than them), they are not willing to risk allowing us to make that choice. So they use the power of our law enforcement, our criminal justice system, and the national security state as a weapon to stop us from exercising our freedom.

We can't allow them to get away with this. Our democracy is under attack. It's up to us to save it. We must hold those responsible accountable at the ballot box and send a strong message to leaders in both parties: those who abuse their power and undermine our democracy will not be tolerated.

If we do nothing, however, and turn a blind eye to those weaponizing our criminal justice system against their political opponents and telling us who we are and are not allowed to vote for, it will set a precedent for every election and presidency in the future and our democracy will be finished.

This is not the America my brothers and sisters in uniform and I risk our lives to defend.

Is Today the Day?

In the predawn darkness of January 2005, I was strapped into my seat, the ruby red nylon restraining belts over my shoulders nearly cutting off circulation to my arms. My body armor felt like an extension of my body, and my rifle was in hand. We were packed like sardines facing each other, bouncing through a blackened sky aboard the C-130 that was taking us into Iraq. With the exception of the four turboprops whirring outside the flying metal tube, there was total silence. There was tension in the air. For most of us, this was our first combat deployment. We had trained for months—at Schofield Barracks in Hawaii, in the desert of Fort Bliss's Camp MacGregor, and in the wet swampy air of Fort Polk, Louisiana. One battle drill after another. Endless convoy operations. React to contact. Break contact. React to ambush. React to IED. As a medical unit, we rehearsed over and over what to do in a mass-casualty-producing event. We were ready. But for what, exactly, no one knew for sure.

As the military aircraft began its descent, we could feel it zig and zag, lurching and pitching in a stomach-churning downward corkscrew intended to make sure our aircraft would not be an easy target for RPGs or other weapons. We plummeted through the darkness. The flaps and landing gear deployed. Without any windows or visual reference points outside, we didn't know exactly where or when the ground would come up to reach us. All we knew was, training was over. We were landing at our camp in Iraq, around forty miles north of Baghdad.

As a kid growing up in Hawaii, the thought of serving in the military never crossed my mind. I experienced at a young age that I was happiest when I was serving God and others. It was the small things that taught me this—bringing a smile to someone's face, letting a fellow surfer ride a wave when they'd been struggling to catch one all morning, preparing and giving out food to those who were homeless and hungry in the park. I knew I wanted to follow a path of service with my life—and started with taking care of my community and my home. I was passionate about protecting the beautiful oceans, land, and mountains of our home state. I'd get my friends together and organize beach cleanups, and cofounded an environmental nonprofit as a teenager. But I felt like I wasn't doing enough. I ran for and was elected to the Hawaii

State Legislature at twenty-one years old. The Islamist terrorist attack on 9/11 happened, and like for so many Americans, it changed my life. I raised my right hand and enlisted in the Hawaii National Guard, and volunteered to deploy to Iraq with my fellow soldiers, leaving my seat in the statehouse behind.

As we unloaded the aircraft on that January morning in 2005, the air was brisk and cold. We moved through a brief administrative processing and found the tents where we would be staying. I was assigned to an Army GP Medium tent with eighteen other women, each of us quickly finding a spot to drop our bags and set up our cots. It was late, and I was tired. I curled up in my sleeping bag, rifle by my side, body armor within arm's reach. Within a few hours, we heard sirens sounding, warning of an incoming mortar attack. We threw on our gear, grabbed our rifles, and ran out to the cement bunker. I don't know how much protection it gave us—but this would end up being an almost daily occurrence for the twelve months we were there.

The next morning, I went for a walk around the camp that would be home for the next year. When I came up to the North Gate, one of the busiest for our security patrols, I saw a sign that stopped me in my tracks. It read in big, bold letters: "IS TODAY THE DAY?"

I would see that sign almost every day I was there. It bore into my consciousness. It was a reminder to us all that any day could be our last. It was also a question that I reflected on often: Life is short. My time could come at any moment. Am I making the most of every day, to live my life in service to God and working for the well-being of His children?

Too many of our fellow soldiers who passed through that gate were killed or wounded. Many of us who made the long trip home found our homecoming bittersweet. We mourned the loss of our friends. Our lives had changed. Our world had changed. Nothing would be the same again. When I got home, I had many sleepless nights. What should've been comfortable and familiar seemed different and out of place. There were no mortar attacks, no sirens, no incoming fire. I laid awake, remembering the words on that sign. IS TODAY THE DAY? I resolved to dedicate myself to a sense of renewed purpose—to honor the sacrifices of our fallen comrades, make every day count, and do all that I could to ensure every American could live free and in peace.

IS TODAY THE DAY?

I urge you to reflect on this same question, which is just as true and relevant to us in our lives today as it was for us in a war zone.

Today is the day. We have no time to waste. We live in troubled times. Our nation is bitterly divided. Our future as a republic, as a union, appears bleak. The news—the noise, the insanity, the darkness—is something many of us want to shut out. There are times when all I want to do is grab my surfboard and paddle out into the ocean, or go for a hike in the mountains, and appreciate the peace and majesty of Mother Nature.

But there is too much at stake, in this moment, to put our heads in the sand and go about our lives with blinders on hoping the insanity will fade away. The insanity and threats to our constitutional democracy will not fade away and will only increase unless we stand up and remind those trying to destroy this country that ours is a government of, by, and for the people.

I joined the Democrat Party in Hawaii in 2002 because I saw a party that, at that time, appeared to be the party of the people, a party that valued free speech, welcoming all comers into a big tent where the sharing of diverse opinions and views on issues was encouraged. It was a party that fought for civil liberties and rights, remembering how neighbors and friends were thrown in Japanese internment camps during World War II, their freedoms taken away in an instant. It was a party inspired by JFK and the Reverend Martin Luther King Jr., who showed us what is possible when we as Americans come together.

The party I joined over twenty years ago no longer exists today.

I could no longer remain in today's Democrat Party, which is now under the complete control of an elitist cabal of warmongers fueled by cowardly wokeness who divide us by racializing every issue and stoke anti-white racism, actively work to undermine our God-given freedoms enshrined in our Constitution, are hostile to people of faith and spirituality, demonize the police and protect criminals at the expense of law-abiding Americans, allow our borders to remain open while claiming they are "secure," weaponize the national security state to go after political opponents, and, above all, drag us closer to nuclear war with each passing day.

Aloha

I left the Democrat Party and became an Independent. For the sake of our country, peace, freedom, and our hope for a prosperous future, I urge you to do the same.

As we look to the way ahead and how we will forge our path through the darkness and toward a brighter future for all Americans, the spirit of aloha serves as the torch that will guide us through.

What is aloha? While you may be familiar with "aloha" as a word often used as a greeting, it means so much more than that.

The word *alo* means to share, and *ha* refers to the eternal life force within each of us. Aloha recognizes that we are all connected in a spiritual sense, as children of God. Knowing this truth inspires how we should relate to each other and how we can come together to defend our God-given freedoms enshrined in the Constitution against those who seek to take them away. While in this book I detail the reasons I left the Democrat Party, and the serious threat the Democrat elite pose to our freedom and democracy in this very moment, I recognize that the challenges we face in our political system and country are not limited to one political party.

Politicians from both political parties who are more interested in serving their own interests than in serving the needs of the American people have taken control of our country. They will not give up their power without a fight.

We live in the greatest country in the world, filled with potential for us to build a brighter future and a more perfect union where every American can live free, in peace, and with opportunity for prosperity . . . a future where we celebrate free speech and respect each other as children of God and as Americans, even if we disagree on an issue or policy. This is the country our Founders envisioned for us, and it is my fervent hope that we come together, remembering the foundational principles that connect us as Americans, to make that vision a reality. It's up to us—all of us—to make it happen.

Will you join me?
Aloha.

CHAPTER ONE

The End of Our Democracy?

I can no longer remain in a party that abuses its power by leveraging the national security state and law enforcement against their opponents, undermining the rule of law and turning our democracy into a banana republic.

O ur democracy can survive only if the United States is firmly rooted on the foundation of the rule of law, a nation where justice is applied equally and fairly, no matter your politics, sex, race, or religion. Guided by their belief that the end justifies the means, the Democrat elite are using the power of law enforcement to target political or personal opponents, undermining the essence of the rule of law and exposing their contempt for the American people and our democracy. If we allow this to continue, the America we know and love will disappear forever. This is why I left the Democrat Party and urge other Democrats who love our country to do the same.

A Nail in the Coffin of Democracy

On June 9, 2023, Biden administration special counsel Jack Smith indicted former president Donald Trump on thirty-seven felony counts based on Smith's investigation into Trump's handling of classified documents after he left the White House. The indictment alleged crimes related to the retention of national defense information, violations of the Espionage Act, obstruction of justice, and false statements.

This was an unprecedented moment in American history. Never before in our country has a sitting president used the powers of law enforcement to criminally indict the political opponent who poses the greatest threat to his reelection bid. This action by the Biden administration is a serious blow to our democracy with aftershocks likely to be felt for decades to come. Will future administrations follow suit? Why wouldn't they? The precedent has been set.

I was in Colorado Springs, wrapping up Army duty as a Civil Affairs Battalion Commander at Fort Carson, when Smith held his press conference. It just so happened I had previously been scheduled to speak at the Western Conservative Summit in Denver the next day. As I made the ninety-minute drive to Denver, I listened to the so-called pundits' commentary on the different cable news networks. While almost all said they recognized the seriousness of what had just occurred, it was obvious that the commentators on networks like CNN and MSNBC could barely contain their glee—finally, Donald J. Trump, their Enemy Number One for so many years, was going to go down. In their minds, victory was at hand.

Once I got to the hotel in Denver, I sat down to prepare for the next day's speech. I took one look at the notes I had written and threw them in the trash. I sat at my laptop to write a new speech that would express the gravity and significance of this moment, not just for the upcoming 2024 election, but for a generation to come.

I began my speech, saying:

> It is a historic and dark day in America—a sitting President of the United States has taken unprecedented action, abusing his power by directing the government and justice system to be used against his major political opponent, charging him with multiple crimes, right in the middle of a competitive presidential campaign, with the election right around the corner. This could be one of the final nails in the coffin of our democracy.
>
> President Biden likes to tell us how he is a champion of democracy. But his actions tell a very different story. With his administration's indictment of President Trump, and their ongoing efforts to target political opponents and limit free speech, their actions remind us more of authoritarian regimes where leaders often use the power of the state to silence or eliminate their opposition.

The heart of a functioning justice system is this: If a law is going to be enforced, it should be enforced equally and fairly across the board.

The Democrat elite and their propaganda arm in the media clearly do not believe in this principle; or more likely, they care more about power than they do about our country and our democracy. The blatant double standard in their application of justice is obvious. There is one standard for the Democrat elite and their cabal of friends in the media, Big Tech, and the national security state, and another standard for anyone who is not a part of their club—especially former president Donald Trump.

As I looked at the accusations against Trump and heard the Democrat elite and propaganda media say over and over, "No one is above the law," I would've laughed at their hypocrisy if the consequences weren't so serious. The reality is, they pick and choose who is and is not "above the law." I remembered watching President Obama's FBI director, James Comey, deliver a lengthy speech during his press conference about his investigation into Hillary Clinton, detailing her vast mishandling of highly classified national security documents in her emails, personal server, laptops, and so forth. His statement was so compelling and damning that I thought, for sure, the investigation would result in an indictment of some sort. But it did not. Comey chose not to prosecute. I shouldn't have been surprised. Hillary Clinton is at the heart of permanent Washington and therefore, to them, is above the law.

Even as Jack Smith's investigation into Trump was ongoing, President Biden was found to be storing in unsecure locations classified documents related to national security. When initially asked about the documents, he told reporters, "I think you're going to find there's nothing there." But there was something there. A whole lot of something. Multiple searches resulted in the discovery of classified documents at his private office, boxed up in his garage in Wilmington, and in his home. Attorney General Merrick Garland appointed Special Counsel Robert Hur to investigate Biden. In a report dated February 5, 2024, Special Counsel Hur stated on page one of the executive summary,[1]

> Our investigation uncovered evidence that President Biden willfully retained and disclosed classified materials after his vice presidency when he was a private citizen. These materials included (1) marked classified documents about military and foreign policy in Afghanistan, and (2) notebooks containing Mr. Biden's handwritten entries about issues of

national security and foreign policy implicating sensitive intelligence sources and methods. FBI agents recovered these materials from the garage, offices, and basement den in Mr. Biden's Wilmington, Delaware home. However, for the reasons summarized below, we conclude that the evidence does not establish Mr. Biden's guilt beyond a reasonable doubt. Prosecution of Mr. Biden is also unwarranted based on our consideration of the aggravating and mitigating factors set forth in the Department of Justice's Principles of Federal Prosecution. For these reasons, we decline prosecution of Mr. Biden.

No consequences. Like Hillary Clinton, President Biden is also above the law. Former president Trump, however, is not part of their permanent Washington club—in fact, he is a threat to their power, and therefore faces the full force of the law.

One of Jack Smith's allegations against President Trump is that he lied to federal agents. This is one of those charges that the Democrat elite use selectively and only against their opponents. During the Obama administration's reign, former director of national intelligence James Clapper and former director of the CIA John Brennan both lied under oath to the U.S. Congress, and not only did they not face prosecution, they kept their jobs and have now been elevated by the Democrat elite and propaganda media who tout them as two of the greatest national security minds in America.

There has also been no accountability for the fifty-one former senior intelligence officials and CIA operatives who orchestrated a baseless, false public statement at the behest of the Biden campaign alleging the contents of Hunter Biden's laptop to be "Russian disinformation" just to keep voters from seeing its contents before we cast our votes in 2020.

Similarly, even in the wake of the Durham Report exposing that the FBI had launched a years-long investigation into Trump based on what they knew were lies, undermining his presidency, no one has been held accountable in any way.

As I detailed these examples to the Western Conservative Summit audience that night in Denver, they recognized the seriousness of the threat we face. What's happening is so much bigger than Trump or any single individual.

We are undergoing a direct assault on our democracy. The Democrat elite and Washington establishment are terrified that we, the people, may make the "wrong" choice in this election by voting for Donald Trump. They are also trying to clamp down on free speech, censoring or limiting certain voices or information that could potentially influence us to make the "wrong" choice. This is the hallmark of a dictatorship, no matter how well-intentioned the Democrat elite claim to be. It is exactly this kind of abuse of power that our Founders wanted to prevent, and why they created the Bill of Rights, emphasizing our right to free speech, freedom of the press, freedom of religion, and freedom of expression.

If this is allowed to continue, the harm inflicted on our country and our democracy may be irreversible.

The Birth of the Big Hoax

For months before the 2016 election, many of my former Democrat colleagues had been breathlessly claiming that Donald Trump was the most racist, unqualified, vile person who had ever sought the office of the presidency. To create suspicion in the minds of the American people about him, they invented a conspiracy theory that he was "colluding" with the Russians to win the election. Hillary Clinton used a similar tactic against me when I ran for president in 2020, accusing me of being "groomed by the Russians." Leading Democrats asserted with great confidence that this theory about Trump was true, and that it was only a matter of time before the evidence was revealed. The fact that there was no evidence didn't stop every mainstream media organization in the country from referring to "Russia collusion" as if it were a matter of settled fact. On October 31, 2016, for instance, the website *Slate* posted a story claiming that Donald Trump had improper ties to Alfa Bank, one of the most powerful financial institutions in Russia.[2]

The problem? None of it was true. As the world learned in May 2022, the story was nothing more than a piece of "opposition research" planted by the Hillary Clinton campaign. According to sworn testimony provided by Robby Mook, who managed the Clinton campaign, Hillary Clinton had overseen a plan to take this fake story, alert the FBI about it, and plant it with a friendly journalist to sow confusion and suspicion about Donald Trump's relationship with Russia.

The *Wall Street Journal* summarized the revelations, saying that "the Clinton campaign created the Trump-Alfa allegation, fed it to a credulous press that failed to confirm the allegations but ran with them anyway, then promoted the story as if it were legitimate news. The campaign also delivered the claims to the FBI, giving journalists another excuse to portray the accusations as serious and perhaps true."[3]

This process of creating fake news, planting it with the "Deep State" (made up of active and retired officials from within the Justice Department and other national security agencies), and handing it over to the media to repeat and amplify, has played itself out over and over again.

The whole point is to mislead the American people and discourage them from voting for Trump. This is what happened with the infamous Steele Dossier, a packet of opposition research put together by British spy-for-hire Christopher Steele, which contained lurid accusations about Russian prostitutes urinating on a bed while Donald Trump watched, among other disgusting things. For years these absurd lies were treated with the utmost seriousness, and not just by the Clinton campaign and other top Democrats. It was used to obtain a FISA warrant to illegally surveil Carter Page, an American citizen, even though the FBI knew full well that it was a shoddy piece of political opposition research. It was revealed publicly that this dossier was nothing more than gossip and rumor from a former associate of Steele's, and yet no one involved in creating the dossier or spreading it was held to account. No apologies or corrections were made by politicians or their friends in the propaganda media who repeated the lie.

The unfortunate reality is that the dirty tactics used by Hillary Clinton, Biden, and the DNC, working hand in glove with their cabal of powerful partners (mainstream media, Big Tech, and the national security state), are very effective. These tactics actually work, which is why they keep using them.

To this day, most Democrats still believe that Donald Trump and his campaign colluded with Vladimir Putin to win the 2016 election, *even though we know for a fact that this was Clinton campaign disinformation.*

When Hillary Clinton told David Axelrod on his podcast in October 2019,[4] while I was running for president of the United States, that I was a Russian asset and that the Russians were "grooming" me, people believed her. The propaganda media repeated Clinton's lies over and over, without ever asking for evidence or fact-checking her themselves. The more they repeated the lie, the more people believed it was the truth.

Around that time, I visited a local Democrat county meeting in a rural South Carolina town for their monthly get-together. I was the only presidential candidate there and took the opportunity to speak to the small group that was gathered there and share a little about myself and why I was running for president. I started walking around meeting people individually after the formal program was finished, and all were welcoming and kind. As I was about to leave, the county chair pulled me aside and asked if she could speak with me for a minute. She was an older African American woman who was clearly the most influential person in the room. She ran a tight ship, and I could see that no one wanted to get on her bad side. As we took a few steps away from the crowd, she gently put her hands on both of my shoulders and looked intently into my eyes. I returned her gaze and saw in her kind eyes that something serious was really bothering her. She said, "Tulsi, I need you to tell me the truth. Are you really working for Putin?"

This was such an insane question to ask—I have served our country in uniform for over twenty years and continue to serve to this day, deployed to war zones, willing to die for America. When she asked me this question, I was a member of the Armed Services and Foreign Affairs Committees in Congress. I attended high-level classified briefings on an almost weekly basis, helping to make decisions impacting our military and the safety and security of the American people.

Yet here we were, in a small town in rural South Carolina, and this woman was deeply troubled by the lies that former secretary of state Hillary Clinton and the media had told her and the American people about me, without any evidence or facts to back up their insane accusation—that I was a traitor, a puppet for Putin, working for Russia against the United States.

I put my hands on her shoulders, looked her straight in the eye, and said, "I love our country so much that I am willing to put my life on the line to defend our nation and the safety, security, and freedom of the American people. Does that answer your question?" She almost had tears in her eyes as relief washed over her face. She smiled slightly, now at ease, and said, "Yes, thank you," and gave me a big hug.

I was glad that she had asked me directly, but as I left the event and got in the car, I felt so disheartened. I knew there were many more people out there just like her who believed Hillary Clinton's lies, and I couldn't reach them all. I didn't have the resources to take on the Hillary Clinton–led Democrat elite machine and their propaganda media Big Tech conglomerate. I was a sitting duck facing their vast arsenal of weaponry.

Years have passed since I suspended my campaign for the presidency, yet I still meet people from all walks of life who continue to believe and repeat Hillary Clinton's insane accusation. This is how deeply the Democrat elite have poisoned our democracy with the rot of their lies.

Regardless of what you may think of Donald Trump, the lengths that the Democrat elite are willing to go to destroy him or anyone they see as their opposition, should concern every American, not only because it is wrong, but because of the precedent it sets. Today it is Donald Trump, the main obstacle to President Biden's 2024 reelection ambitions, who is being prosecuted by Biden's Department of Justice and FBI. Tomorrow, the tables may turn, and it could be a Democrat who is on the receiving end.

If we allow presidents to use the power and might of the government to take down their political opponents, America will become no better than a banana republic, where each new election is essentially a revolution, with the outgoing administration subject to punishment and former presidents forced to flee the country to avoid getting locked up by the victors.

When most news organizations reported the case against Donald Trump in New York, they did so under the simple headline "Trump Indicted."[5] Some included a brief subhead about how the indictment involved former president Trump's payment of "hush money" to the porn star Stormy Daniels. What most of them *didn't* say, however, is that the underlying crime for which Alvin Bragg and his office had decided to indict the former president was, under New York law, a misdemeanor.

Alvin Bragg, who had campaigned for the office of district attorney promising to "get Trump" *on something*, had finally figured out a way to fulfill his campaign promise. Given the harm it would inflict on the former president, and the accolades he would get for being the first prosecutor to indict Donald Trump, he wouldn't allow a simple thing like the rule of law get in his way.

Bragg used the law to go after political opponents while turning a blind eye to criminals creating anarchy on the streets of New York. One of his first acts as Manhattan District Attorney was to send a memo to his staff advising them not to seek jail time or bail for many serious crimes, including assault. As a result, the rate of serious crimes went up by 22 percent within his first year in office.[6] The people of New York City can't get on the subway or walk down the street without being at risk of being the next victim of a crime specifically because of Bragg's decision to prosecute political opponents instead of violent criminals. Unfortunately, this is not happening only in New York City. There are other DAs and prosecutors just like Bragg who have been put in power by the Democrat elite in cities across the country and empowered criminals to rule the streets.

Divider in Chief

In March of 2020, all but three Democrat candidates had suspended their campaigns for the presidency—Joe Biden, Bernie Sanders, and myself. At that point, I had heard that Bernie Sanders was just days away from endorsing Biden, so it was clear to me that the primary election was basically over. Knowing Biden would be the nominee, I suspended my campaign and endorsed him, concluding that this would provide the best, and probably only, opportunity for me to be in a position to try to influence him to listen to his better angels, stick to his promise to unite our country, and reject the warmongering voices clamoring for regime-change wars, a new Cold War, and a nuclear arms race. Unfortunately, he chose the path of darkness.

Two years later, on September 1, 2022, at 8:00 p.m. President Biden stood before Independence Hall in Philadelphia to deliver a speech billed as "The Battle for the Soul of the Nation." The symbolism of choosing to deliver this speech at the place where our Founders debated and adopted the Declaration of Independence and U.S. Constitution was significant. It was a powerful opportunity for the president to inspire the American people to unite around the fundamental principles of freedom enshrined in our Constitution that defines us, not as Democrats or Republicans, but as Americans.

Well, he did invoke our Founders' vision and the principles that serve as a bedrock for our country, but not in a unifying call to work together to serve the interests of all the American people.

Instead—with midterm elections just two months away—he chose to use that hallowed ground to divide us by stoking the fires of hate among his supporters.

When I turned the television on to watch the speech, the imagery I saw was jarring, to say the least. There was Joe Biden, flanked by Marines in dress uniform, silhouetted by ominous red lighting behind them. It looked like that scene from so many movies where the villain takes the stage to announce he is taking over the world by force, and if we do not comply, we will pay the price.

But this wasn't a Hollywood movie set.

This was the president of the United States addressing the nation, looking into the camera and declaring that the greatest threat to democracy and the United States of America was roughly 73 million of my fellow Americans who didn't vote for him.

Biden warned, "Donald Trump and the MAGA Republicans represent an extremism that threatens the very foundations of our republic." He continued, "The Republican Party today is dominated, driven, and intimidated by Donald Trump and the MAGA Republicans, and that is a threat to this country."[7]

He was talking about Americans. My fellow Americans.

Never before in the history of our country has a president so directly labeled tens of millions of Americans as traitors and enemies of the nation. This is the kind of thing we expect from a tyrant, not the president of the greatest democracy in the world.

Demonizing political opponents isn't anything new. President Obama had mocked conservatives, saying they "cling to guns or religion or antipathy to people who aren't like them."[8] Hillary Clinton took this a step further, saying that *these* people—Trump supporters—belonged in a "basket of deplorables."

But Joe Biden escalated these attacks to a whole new level by declaring the deplorables to be not only extremists, but the greatest threat to the United States of America. As such, Biden has now directed all the power of the mightiest law enforcement apparatus and national security state in the world to defeat this supposed threat.

The Biden-controlled law enforcement and national security state wasted no time taking action.

Anyone who opposes the Democrat elite's woke agenda and ideology is demonized by being labeled a "MAGA Republican." In addition to declared supporters of President Trump, it includes the Moms for Liberty who are fighting for the right of parents to have a say in their child's education; it includes unaffiliated voters who are speaking out in opposition to biological males competing against girls in sports; it includes people who dare to question or oppose the warmongers in Washington who are pushing us into Cold Wars with Russia and China, and closer to the brink of nuclear catastrophe; it includes those who are calling for secure borders and support for our police to keep our streets safe.

In short, the Democrats' sights are set on commonsense-minded Americans from across the political spectrum who care about their children, our democracy, and our security and are not afraid to stand up against the insanity of the Democrat elite's agenda.

The Democrat elite are executing a well-thought-out, calculated strategy. They know that once they name and define an enemy, and word goes out that a certain group of people is the target, anything is permissible. Anyone can criticize and spout lies about Trump, the so-called "MAGA Republicans" or the "deplorables," and no one in the mainstream media will push back or challenge the assertion. To the contrary, they will promote and amplify your voice. But if you dare to challenge the mainstream establishment narrative, or God forbid, speak up in support of Donald Trump, they will do all they can to smear and silence you, enlisting the help of their friends in the media and Big Tech.

The Democrat elite don't believe in free speech. They don't believe in the full exercise of the freedoms guaranteed to every one of us under the Bill of Rights. They, and they alone, get to determine which rights we are allowed to have and which rights they will curtail to serve their interests. In curtailing those rights, they do not hesitate to use all levers of power under their control to force compliance.

Our Founding Fathers envisioned that our nation would be a country of laws, not men, and that our government agencies, institutions, and law enforcement would be nonpartisan and unbiased, rising above party politics. The Democrat elites' politicizing of agencies like the FBI, DOJ, DHS, IRS, and even the DOE to harass and intimidate their political opponents is completely undermining the rule of law and therefore, our democracy. This is draining any trust the American people may have had that our government exists to serve the interests of the people, not of those in power. The Democrat elite don't care. The only thing they care about is power.

Toward the end of President Obama's first term, the Internal Revenue Service was exposed for maintaining a blacklist of "right-wing" conservative groups that had applied for nonprofit status. Those on the list were blocked, slow-rolled, or targeted for harassment. When I first heard about this, I didn't believe it. I thought it was some overblown complaint or a story made up by President Obama's opponents to cause him political harm. For all of its faults, and there are many, the IRS is supposed to be neutral, to treat every American the same, and in particular to treat all who apply for nonprofit status the same, no matter our political views, religion, or race. I thought, there's no way the IRS under President Obama would be so bold in abusing their power as to target and harass Obama's political opponents. If they were, this would be an egregious breach of the power the IRS has been entrusted with.

I started digging into this issue and doing some research, learning more about the nonprofits that were being targeted. I was shocked. The IRS wasn't targeting them because they were groups trying to revive the KKK, or incite violence or harm to others. The IRS was targeting organizations that had the word "Patriot" or "Tea Party" in their names. President Obama was, indeed, using the IRS to go after his political opposition.

At the time, Democrat leaders in Washington tried to dismiss the IRS scandal as a "conspiracy theory"—but they were oddly silent when the IRS itself, once caught, admitted its wrongdoing and apologized for its abuse of power.

It doesn't end there. The Treasury Department sent a letter to U.S. Senator Tim Scott in February 2024 admitting to surveilling Americans' personal financial transactions after January 6, 2021, without a warrant or due process,[9] violating the Fourth Amendment which protects our right to privacy against "unreasonable searches" by the government. This was driven by Treasury's Financial Crimes Enforcement Network (FinCEN), warning financial institutions to look out for "extremist indicators," citing as examples "the purchase of books (including religious texts)" like the Bible, and those who shop at stores like Cabela's, Dick's Sporting Goods, and Bass Pro Shops. The Biden administration was specifically looking for Americans' transactions that included Zelle payments with keywords like "MAGA," "Trump," and more.

This is one of many examples of how agencies within the federal government are being used for politically motivated attacks and unconstitutional surveillance of our personal lives, setting a dangerous precedent that undermines our constitutional republic.

We have seen this story before, and we know how it ends. These are textbook tactics the Democrat elite uses to abuse their power and undermine the rule of law just to get what they want. With every offense they get away with, they become more blatant and emboldened in how far they're willing to go to get more power. They are convinced they are above the law, accountable to no one. In their minds, they are untouchable.

Guilty until Proven Innocent

On March 30, 2022, shortly after it was announced that a grand jury in New York would indict former president Donald Trump over alleged hush money payments he made to a porn star, Nancy Pelosi tweeted:

> The Grand Jury has acted upon the facts and the law.
> No one is above the law, and everyone has the right to a trial
> to prove innocence.
> Hopefully, the former President will peacefully respect the
> system, which grants him that right.[10]

What? Come again?
"Everyone has the right to a trial to prove innocence."
Prove *innocence*?

Nancy Pelosi has served in Congress for over thirty-six years and as Speaker of the House twice. And yet she seems not to know a pillar foundational tenet of our justice system—that everyone is innocent until proven guilty. A child who has taken a basic civics class in grade school could tell you this—or anyone who has seen an episode of *Law & Order* on television.

I served in Congress with Nancy Pelosi for eight years. I've seen her in action and can tell you firsthand, Nancy Pelosi is many things, but she is not stupid. She held on to the reins of leadership for so long because she is calculating, strategic, and intentional in every decision she makes. She misses nothing. The only logical explanation for her statement I can see is that she was saying the quiet part out loud. She let slip out what she and the Democrat elite really believe: when it comes to Donald J. Trump, the rule of law does not apply. For years they've told the American people that former president Trump is guilty of *something*—apparently the plan was that they'd figure out which *something* they could get him on later.

This approach isn't new. The Democrat elite are implementing a tactic used by Stalin's longest-serving secret police chief, Lavrentiy Beria, who famously said, "Show me the man and I'll show you the crime."

If they can get away with this against President Donald Trump, Biden's most prominent political opponent, they can do it to any of us. And they are. They use all the tools and powers at their disposal to go after anyone who does not submit to their will—whether it be a business, a nonprofit, or an individual. There are a plethora of laws at the federal, state, and local levels, many of them out of date, no longer necessary, and rarely if ever, used. But they are still on the books, allowing those in power to find a crime to fit just about anyone in any circumstance. "Show me the man and I'll show you the crime."

They also use the threat of law enforcement to intimidate us into submission. When the FBI comes calling, most people feel compelled to comply, knowing that there will likely be consequences if they do not. The release of the Twitter Files exposed how the FBI bullied the social media platform into censoring Americans that the Biden administration did not want to have a voice. The IRS has been weaponized against people and organizations, has harassed them and buried them in investigations, audits, and paperwork. Even the EPA has the power to destroy a business by finding some arcane environmental policy and applying it in a way that can bring a business to an immediate halt.

This is not "conspiracy theory," a hypothesis, or a warning about the future—this is happening in the United States today.

In the minds of the Democrat elite, they themselves are the good guys, and anyone who does not submit to their wishes are the bad guys.

And the bad guys are, as Nancy Pelosi let slip, guilty until proven innocent.

Worse yet, they are guilty even if the facts prove their innocence.

I have gone into just a few examples of how the Democrat elite and Washington establishment are trying to destroy Donald Trump, and are willing to sacrifice our democracy and country in the process. I could write a whole book detailing all they have thrown and continue to throw at him. Regardless of how you feel about Donald J. Trump or his policies, you have to wonder how it is that he has endured years of attacks, lawsuits, betrayal, and the full force of the judicial system and national security state working against him during his presidency and his campaign. I've known many strong, tough people in my life, but I can't think of a single one who could not only withstand these pressures without crumbling, but actually choose to keep fighting against the entire Washington establishment swamp. Do you think Joe Biden could handle this? I know Joe Biden and used to consider him a friend. He would crumble under just 5 percent of the pressure, stress, and attacks that Trump has endured. I've met with Donald Trump and spoken to him at length. I've witnessed his heartfelt interactions, away from the cameras, with veterans and friends of mine. I've gotten a sense for what his motives are—and they have nothing to do with what the Washington establishment accuses him of. He's a fighter whose strength and resilience comes from a sincere concern for the future of our country and his care for the American people.

Broad Discretion

In a society that is based on law and order, we expect those entrusted to keep us safe to do their jobs. If we don't feel safe in our homes or communities, then we no longer have the right to "life, liberty, and the pursuit of happiness" that the Declaration of Independence guarantees. While the Democrat elite eagerly undermine the rule of law to go after political opponents, they choose not to enforce the laws at our border to secure our country and stop illegal immigrants from entering. A president who fails to secure our nation has failed at his most fundamental responsibility. Without secure borders, we have no country.

Due to the Biden administration's failure to fulfill its responsibility to secure our borders, Texas Governor Greg Abbott has invoked the constitutional right of states to defend themselves, and taken action to secure the border in his home state. Rather than applauding his efforts, the Biden administration is doing all they can to stop him. They have taken down the barriers he put in place, cut holes in concertina wire to allow illegal migrants into our country, filed lawsuits to try to get the courts to stop him, and normalized the "catch and release" policy leaving millions of illegal migrants in our country with no means of tracking or enforcement. This is not just a Texas problem or an Arizona problem—it's a national crisis. The House Committee on Homeland Security reported more than 2.4 million encounters at the southwest border in 2023 alone, and more than 3.2 million encounters nationwide—the worst ever in history. New records of immigrants illegally crossing our border are being set as I write this book. Meanwhile, those who try to follow our immigration laws and apply for visas to come and visit loved ones or to come to America to start a new business and create jobs are either rejected or often wait years just to get their applications processed.

This is a national security crisis and a humanitarian crisis. Many people trying to illegally cross our border are trying to escape hardship and suffering in their home country. Many of them have risked their lives during their journey to our border. While we have compassion for them, we must be grounded in reality. We do not have the capacity or resources to help every person in the world who is suffering and would like to come to the United States to seek a better life. We have veterans living on our streets, rising homelessness, contaminated water, crumbling infrastructure, and many other dire needs that our government must work to address for our own citizens. Those who wish to come to our country must respect and follow our laws.

The Biden-Harris administration has lied to Congress and the American people for over three years, promising that the border is secure. They assume we are too stupid to see what's really going on. I've been to the border and seen the huge gaps where illegal immigrants can easily walk through. I've walked through the border communities that have been most directly impacted by this crisis, overwhelmed by the masses of illegal immigrants on the streets. Cities like New York provide housing, food, and most recently a prepaid debit card for illegal immigrant families.[11] Elderly veterans have been tossed out of their housing to make room for illegal immigrants.[12] With the rise of illegal immigration has come an increase in crime. The negative effects of Biden's open border policies are impacting all parts of our country and are undermining our national security as millions of people stroll across our southern border completely unvetted. When Hezbollah operatives

Ali Kourani and Samar el-Debek were arrested in the United States on terrorism charges, they exposed Hezbollah's plan: develop a network of sleeper cells across North America that can be activated at any time. Hezbollah is carrying out this plan, and it is not the only Islamist terrorist group lying in wait for an opportunity to launch a catastrophic attack against Americans on our soil.

It is imperative that we understand the goal of Islamist jihadists, which is the same whether they call themselves Hamas, Hezbollah, ISIS, al-Qaeda or one of the many other Islamist terrorist groups: to kill or enslave the "infidels" or nonbelievers, wherever they may be. As absurd as it sounds, the reality is that radical Islamist jihadists are steadfast in their belief that Allah will reward them in heaven for killing all who reject their radical brand of Islam—whether they're Jews, Christians, Hindus, or Muslims. Such fanatics celebrate death and are emboldened to martyr themselves and others in the process of killing "nonbelievers" because they are convinced their rape and slaughter of God's children who don't share their insane ideology will be rewarded in heaven.

The most recent example of this was the heinous attack launched by Hamas in Israel on October 7, 2023, killing over 1,200 innocent Israeli men, women, and children. This was not just the latest battle in the decades-long conflict between Israel and Palestine. It is the most recent front in the greater war being waged by Sunni and Shia Islamist jihadists throughout the world. It should be a wake-up call to leaders everywhere that Islamist jihadists are the greatest short- and long-term threat to the safety, security, and freedom of the American people, and people throughout the world.

Unfortunately, President Biden and Democrat leaders refuse to recognize this threat. Afraid of being labeled Islamophobes, they have become captive to Islamist ideologues and jihadi apologists. Instead of focusing on defeating Islamist jihadists like al-Qaeda, President Biden has instead pursued his hypocritical mission of spreading democracy and defeating "dictators," "autocrats," and "communism"—even as the Biden administration undermines our own democracy and rule of law here at home. This shortsightedness and cowardice has empowered Islamist jihadists to strengthen their position in their ongoing global jihad, pursuing their overarching mission of establishing a global Islamist caliphate. The Biden-Harris administration's open border policies lay out the welcome mat, allowing hundreds of thousands, if not millions, of military-aged males from all over the world to illegally stream into our country, increasing the risk and likelihood of a catastrophic attack occurring on our soil.

Knowing all of this, why in the world would the Democrat elite continue their open border policy? Political opportunity. Hispanic and other ethnic minority voters have traditionally voted for Democrats. They figure that the more illegal immigrants Biden allows into the country, the more likely states like Texas that have traditionally voted for Republicans will turn blue, locking in the balance of power in our country in favor of Democrats.

While she made the statement several years ago, Rep. Yvette Clarke (D-NY) said the quiet part out loud, referring to welcoming illegal immigrants into her district: "When I hear colleagues talk about, you know, the doors of the inn being closed—ah, no room at the inn—I'm saying I need more people in my district just for redistricting purposes."[13]

Like many other policies the Democrat elite are pushing that go against the interest of the American people, our safety and well-being, it comes down to how they can increase their stranglehold on power and control of the people.

The Democrat elite couldn't care less about going after the criminals running rampant in cities throughout our country. In fact, just like with illegal immigration, they are promoting policies that protect criminals over law-abiding citizens. In many cities, our children are afraid to ride their bicycles down the street or go out and play at the park. Driving through Washington, D.C., comes with a risk of carjackings that often end in serious injury or murder. I regularly travel to New York City for work, and when I walk down the street, my defenses are always up.

In 2010, I was elected to serve as a member of the Honolulu City Council, representing over 100,000 residents of urban Honolulu. My district was very diverse—including everything from Hawaiian home-steads in Papakolea to historic single-family homes in the back of Nuuanu Valley to skyscrapers in downtown Honolulu. As with many densely populated communities, safety was a foremost concern. As Chair of the Public Safety committee, I worked closely with community leaders and the Honolulu Police Department to find ways to make it so people could feel safe in their homes as they traveled to work and when they walked their kids down the street to play in the park.

At the time, I lived in a studio apartment in downtown Honolulu. I walked about a mile to and from Honolulu Hale, where City Council meetings were held, and appreciated the convenience of living down-town where I could walk to work, or to get fresh produce from the open markets in Chinatown, to the Hawaii State Library, post office, gym, or supermarket. We had many affordable housing apartment units for the elderly located downtown for that same reason. Many of them were living on a limited fixed income, and everything they needed was generally within a few blocks, including the biggest hospital in our state.

Unfortunately, one of the challenges we faced was homeless encampments springing up around urban Honolulu. This was not a new problem. Ever since I was a kid catching the bus to martial arts class or to my job as a cashier at the grocery store, I always had to look over my shoulder and be aware of my surroundings because of a random homeless person who was mentally ill, babbling while walking down the street, or a drug addict passed out in a doorway in Chinatown. But things had gotten much worse. We were now seeing tent cities pop up in highly trafficked areas, taking over entire sidewalks, forcing the elderly and families with children to walk into the streets to get around them, dodging cars and traffic, endangering their lives.

Even as we worked on affordable housing solutions, halfway houses, and mental health providers to help people off the streets and get them the care they needed, the reality was that there was a growing safety hazard to pedestrians. Police officers were frustrated because they had no legal authority to do anything about it. Working with community leaders and stakeholders, I introduced and passed Bill 54, which essentially made it illegal to store private property on public sidewalks and thoroughfares—whether you're homeless or not.[14] This provided a necessary tool for police officers to begin clearing the sidewalks, and a way for service providers to help people transition off the street and into some form of shelter, housing, or care. And it worked. Sidewalks that were previously impassable for pedestrians, including the elderly, were now cleared and safe for all to traverse. Parks that had become unusable and unsafe because they had turned into homeless encampments were restored to a state where kids felt safe and welcome to come and play after school. Small business owners were happy because open sidewalks brought more foot traffic and customers to their shops.

However, this bill aroused strong opposition from so-called progressive activists, many in the Occupy movement, who called my legislation "cruel and unusual punishment." They complained that it would take away the only place where homeless people could "survive rent free" on the island. Apparently, they didn't care about the seventy-five-year-old woman who can no longer care for herself because she doesn't feel safe walking to the store to pick up her medicine and food. Or the mother who has to push her baby in a stroller on the street toward oncoming traffic because the sidewalk has been taken over by a wall-to-wall tent city. They were not concerned about getting people off the streets who need help and into transitional housing, or placing those who were mentally ill and posed a risk to others into facilities where they can be safe, or about making our community safe by locking up criminals.

Our experience in Honolulu is being felt in many cities across the country. It has become common for the most "woke" people in today's Democrat Party—the same ones who will tell you with a straight face that using the wrong pronoun or uttering an offensive phrase is "*literally* violence"—to downplay acts of *actual* violence when they occur. Rather than address the real challenges in law enforcement and the broken criminal justice system, rather than come up with grassroots-driven policies to reduce crime in urban neighborhoods, these so-called progressives have decided to "defund the police" and treat victims of crime like perpetrators and criminals like victims. The result? Fewer violent criminals end up behind bars, and more violent crimes occur on our streets.

These people are essentially anarchists who don't care about other people. They don't believe in the rule of law, and apparently couldn't care less about ensuring safety, peace, and order in our communities.

Shortly after the death of George Floyd, Democrats and Republicans alike denounced his killing. There were massive protests across the country and around the world that called for "racial justice." Many of these protests devolved into violent riots, where roving mobs effectively took over control of some American cities, including Seattle and Portland, leaving police overwhelmed and powerless to stop the violence. In some places, the mayors of these cities told the police to stand down. Do nothing. Among the Democrat elite, this anarchy was applauded by some and met with silence by others.

Amid this crisis, I and others saw a unique window of opportunity to pass meaningful reforms that could help support our law

enforcement and prevent the rare, but tragic, incidents of police brutality. I worked with my friend Senator Tim Scott and others on
thoughtful and comprehensive police reform legislation that brought
together Democrats, Republicans, and criminal justice reform advocates. Not surprisingly, the House Democrats put together competing legislation, because there was no way in hell they would allow
a Republican-sponsored bill on police reform to pass. That was not
good politics for them, and power was (and is) more important to
them than passing legislation that could lead to real positive change.

Once Tim Scott's bill was slated to come up for a vote in the House
of Representatives, I received an email alert from the House Democratic
Caucus notifying all Democrat members of an emergency conference
call to discuss the legislation and the plan to move forward. I sat there
with my phone on speaker, listening to one Democrat Party leader
after another rage against the Scott legislation and express strong support for the House Democrats bill. They didn't mention that Scott's
legislation included roughly 70 percent of the reforms that Democrats
had been calling for, and most importantly, that his bill would likely
pass both the House and Senate and be signed into law, whereas many
Republicans felt the House Democrats' bill went too far and would
not support it.

The thing that stuck with me from that conference call was when
the House Democrat leadership made the case for passing their legislation by saying they wanted to show their donors and supporters that
they are actually "doing something" about police reform—omitting the
fact that their legislation would be dead on arrival in the Senate and
therefore would do nothing at all—it was all for show. Nothing would
change. They weren't interested in actually fixing the problem. All they
cared about was scoring cheap political points.

So instead of doing anything to fix the problem, they went ahead
with their demonize-and-defund-the-police plan. The fact that the

Democrat elite rallied behind the preposterous idea of getting rid of law enforcement shows just how out of touch with reality they really are, and how content they are to surrender to crime and anarchy. On June 12, 2020, the *New York Times* ran an op-ed by Mariame Kaba titled "Yes, We Mean Literally Abolish the Police: Because Reform Won't Happen." In this piece, which is refreshing for its honesty, if nothing else, the author wrote,

> Enough. We can't reform the police. The only way to diminish police violence is to reduce contact between the public and the police.
>
> There is not a single era in United States history in which the police were not a force of violence against black people. . . .
>
> So when you see a police officer pressing his knee into a black man's neck until he dies, that's the logical result of policing in America. When a police officer brutalizes a black person, he is doing what he sees as his job.[15]

This is the lunacy that my former party endorsed, both in policy and with dangerous, harmful, and endless accusations that we as a country, including our police officers, are irredeemably racist.

This was maddening to me because they had no idea what they were talking about. They seemed to live in a little fantasy bubble of an echo chamber where they made things up, nodded with each other in agreement, and patted each other on the back for being so high-minded, self-righteous, and perfect. To this day they slander the very police officers who are charged with securing the U.S. Capitol, whose job it is to keep members of Congress safe. They demonize the officers who patrol our city streets at night, putting their lives at risk to keep others safe. While they are quick to cite abhorrent cases of police brutality, they refuse to honor the countless men and women across America who pay the ultimate price and sacrifice their lives in the line of duty, fulfilling their mission to serve and protect.

When I was in Congress, I attended the annual candlelight vigil held on the National Mall to honor every law enforcement officer who was killed in the line of duty the previous year. As the sun sets and the honor guard marches, with bagpipes playing "Amazing Grace," the families of the fallen start to light their candles. Each flame is small on its own, yet in the hands of tens of thousands of Americans gathered there, the candles light up the night's dark sky for as far as the eye can see. As I stood there with leaders from the Honolulu Police Department and families of fallen officers from Hawaii, my heart ached for the families of every one of the officers whose name was read aloud. I'll never forget holding in my arms the wife of a police officer killed in the line of duty as she wept, her whole body shaking with tears. Or the look in the eyes of a six-year-old girl who didn't quite understand how it was that one day her dad kissed her goodnight as he tucked her into bed, and the next day he was gone, never to come home again.

My sister was a deputy U.S. marshal for eleven years. She served on a Fugitive Task Force, actively tracking and hunting down convicted violent criminals. We felt the anxiety and stress of knowing the risk she faced, kicking down a door where she could be met on the other side with the blast of a shotgun. We prayed every day for her safety and the safety of those she served with.

During my second deployment with the Hawaii National Guard, I served as a platoon leader where the majority of my soldiers worked as police officers in their civilian jobs at home. They were predominantly racial and ethnic minorities who chose this profession as an answer to a higher calling—putting their own lives on the line to serve and protect others, to work for the safety and well-being of their fellow Americans, no matter who they were or what they looked like.

Given the anti-police sentiment of the Democrat elite, you would think they would be vigilant in stopping federal agents from the FBI, DOJ, and other agencies from abusing their power—especially when they are doing so to prevent American citizens from exercising their First Amendment rights. You would think Joe Biden would be extremely wary of using these tactics during his presidency, especially against his political enemies.

If you thought that, you'd be wrong.

Early one morning in September of 2022, the Biden administration sent a team of FBI agents to the home of Mark Houck, a pro-life activist who, a year earlier, had been arrested (though never charged) for getting in a minor scuffle on the sidewalk outside an abortion clinic during a peaceful protest. A jury of Houck's peers decided not to convict him of anything. But that didn't matter to the Biden administration. As Houck and his children were sleeping in their beds, FBI agents barreled through the door with rifles pointed at Houck as they put him in cuffs and hauled him off. It's clear the Biden administration did this to send a message to other peaceful pro-life protestors that if they dare to challenge the "woke" agenda of the Demcrat elite, they too will be punished.[16]

In June of 2021, Scott Smith of Loudon County was arrested for angrily expressing his outrage at the Loudon County school board for their inaction in the wake of his daughter being sexually assaulted in the girl's bathroom by a boy claiming to identify as a girl. Instead of prosecuting the boy and changing the school's policy that allowed boys dressed as girls to use the girls' bathroom, the school took no legal action against the boy, instead quietly transferring him to another school where he went on to sexually assault another girl. What parent wouldn't be outraged at this situation? Instead of working to protect innocent children, the Biden administration's Department of Justice decided to go after parents like Scott Smith, actively directing the FBI's Counterterrorism Division to track parents protesting at school board meetings, citing them as potential domestic terror threats.[17]

Those are just two examples. There are many more that reveal how the Biden administration and the Democrat elite are actively using all of the power at their fingertips, not to protect the safety and security of the American people, but instead to harass, assault, and target everyday Americans who dare to oppose them—everyone from a former president down to a father standing up for his daughter who had been sexually assaulted at school.

The Bottom Line

Our nation's Founders envisioned "a government of laws, not of men," recognizing that the rule of law, with a judicial system separate from the political powers in the government, is fundamental to a free and just society. Being entrusted with the power to uphold the rule of law comes with the grave responsibility of the power of the gun—law enforcement. We must be able to trust those in power to enforce the law in a neutral, fair, and just manner, inspired by the blindfolded Lady Justice.

The Democrat elite have betrayed us all by undermining the rule of law, abusing this sacred trust, and turning this power into a weapon directed toward their opponents. They wield this weapon not only against anyone who directly threatens their political power by challenging them in an election, but toward everyday Americans who disagree with them or dare to speak the truth and challenge their authority. Commonsense Americans who believe in our Constitution and the vision our Founders had for America understand that the rule of law is the foundation of a functioning democracy, setting us apart from banana republics and nations ruled by tyrants.

No matter your political affiliation, join me in rejecting this gross abuse of power perpetrated by the Democrat elite, who are willing to sacrifice the foundation of who we are as a country to feed their slavish hunger for power. Only by rejecting them can we ensure that our democracy survives and thrives, allowing us to strive toward a "more perfect Union," where each and every American is guaranteed our God-given rights to "life, liberty, and the pursuit of happiness."

CHAPTER TWO

Fading Light of Freedom

The Democrat elite, once dedicated to defending freedom and civil liberties, are now undermining both, acting as "Big Brother," using the long arm of government to control every part of our lives.

As they constructed our founding documents, our Founding Fathers understood that their most important task was to contain government power and protect individual rights and liberty. The individual rights that our nation's framers knew they must protect from government abuse or control are what they referred to in the Declaration of Independence as "unalienable rights."

"We hold these truths to be self-evident, that all men are created equal, that they are endowed, by their Creator, with certain unalienable rights, that among these are life, liberty, and the pursuit of happiness."

James Madison, often called the Father of the Constitution, referred to these "natural" rights as "the great rights of mankind"—intrinsic to every one of us as human beings—because he understood that they are endowed to us *by God*. No person, institution, or government entity can take away these natural unalienable rights. Contrary to what many may believe, the Bill of Rights was not written to bestow upon us certain rights and freedoms; it was written specifically to protect our "unalienable" rights from those in government who may abuse their power and seek to undermine such rights.

Sadly, the very thing our nation's Founders sought to protect us from is happening before our very eyes at the hands of the Democrat elite. They do not respect God, the nature of our unalienable rights, the Constitution, the Bill of Rights, or us—the people—and therefore they have no qualms about undermining our freedoms and civil liberties in their endless pursuit of power. I could no longer call myself a Democrat and be associated with a party that does not believe in our intrinsic freedoms and therefore cannot be trusted to protect them.

Liberty versus Security

Early one morning on the anniversary of the attack on Pearl Harbor, I stepped into the small boat that shuttles visitors to and from the USS *Arizona* Memorial to honor those who were killed on that fateful day. The morning air was crisp, the sky was clear with barely a cloud in sight, huge ships docked at the pier, and American flags were waving at the different naval headquarters on shore. I could see sailors on the ship decks moving about, completing their morning tasks. The breeze was refreshing and the water a beautiful, deep blue. I imagined families waking up to a similar peaceful, quiet morning on Sunday, December 7, 1941. I could almost see the sailors fulfilling their morning duties on the ship deck when, at 7:48 a.m., Japanese kamikaze pilots began their surprise attack on Pearl Harbor, dropping bombs that whistled through the air, landing with catastrophic explosions. Within ninety minutes the Japanese had damaged 19 U.S. warships and 300 aircraft and killed 2,403 American servicemembers. Nearly half of the dead were in the USS *Arizona*, which sank within 9 minutes after a bomb landed on the ship's millions of pounds of ammunition, causing it to explode.

The next day, at 12:30 p.m., President Franklin D. Roosevelt went before a joint session of Congress to ask for a declaration of war. In his six-minute address, which was broadcast live to a nationwide radio audience, he said, "Yesterday, December 7, 1941, a date which will live in infamy, the United States of America was suddenly and deliberately attacked by naval and air forces of the Empire of Japan."

He beseeched Congress to act: "I ask that the Congress declare that since the unprovoked and dastardly attack by Japan on Sunday, December 7, 1941, a state of war has existed between the United States and the Japanese Empire."[1]

The United States was at war. Our nation would never be the same.

Hawaii has a long history of immigrants from Japan and other countries coming to our shores. Many of them came looking for work on the plantations filled with sugarcane and pineapple as far as the eye could see. Between 1860 and 1940, nearly 300,000 Japanese citizens had immigrated to Hawaii and the mainland United States. Most came looking for work, many on multiyear contracts to work on plantations, with plans to return home after their contract was complete. Others decided to stay, raise their families in this country, and live the American dream, starting small shops and businesses with hopes of providing their children with opportunities they never had.

Less than four months after the attack on Pearl Harbor, their lives would radically change. The U.S. government looked at all people of Japanese descent with suspicion, whether they were American citizens or not. Naturally, that skepticism went beyond the government and spread quickly, leading to Japanese Americans and immigrants from Japan facing discrimination and racist attacks. The change happened quickly, almost overnight. People who were friends, neighbors, classmates, and work friends one day, now looked at them with disgust, openly yelled slurs at them, and closed their doors to them when they needed help. They didn't want to be seen as sympathizers with the "dirty Japs."

On February 19, 1942, President Roosevelt issued Executive Order 9066, which empowered the U.S. military to create "relocation centers" to incarcerate those suspected of espionage and deemed a threat to national security.[2] While it was not expressly stated in the order, the intent was clear: these camps were for the "Japs." All Japanese American men who were eligible for the draft were labeled "enemy aliens."

Over the next six months, more than 122,000 men, women, and children across the country were forcibly removed, oftentimes with no notice, from their homes, schools, and places of work, and held against their will in internment camps. Nearly 70,000 of them were American citizens. Overnight, they lost everything—their homes, businesses, savings, and property. Most important, they lost their liberty. They were never charged with a crime, there was no evidence presented, no trial was held, and no avenue for them to appeal their unlawful incarceration.

By the time the war ended, not a single Japanese American or Japanese national residing in the United States had been found guilty of espionage or sabotage.

Despite all of this, roughly 33,000 Japanese Americans volunteered to serve in the U.S. military during and immediately after World War II. Approximately 800 of them sacrificed their lives during this war. Over 10,000 soldiers enlisted to serve in a segregated unit the Army created specifically for ethnic Japanese, the 100th battalion of the 442nd

Infantry Regiment. Four thousand Japanese-speaking volunteers, many of whom came from internment camps in Hawaii and the mainland United States, served in the Military Intelligence Service, deploying and fighting against the Japanese of their parents' homeland.

The motto of the nisei-only 442nd Infantry Regiment was "Go for Broke"—a slang phrase that refers to putting it all on the line.

The 442nd Regiment's "Go for Broke" song goes like this:

Four Forty-Second Infantry: We're the boys from Hawai'i nei. We're fighting for you, and the red, white and blue.[3]

These men knowingly volunteered to go to war, where they were placed directly into heavy combat, putting their own lives in grave danger to defend the United States of America—the same country that saw them as enemy aliens, and that with a stroke of a pen had so egregiously taken away liberty and freedom for those they loved. They endured some of the fiercest combat in World War II and to this day remain the most decorated unit in U.S. military history.[4]

It wasn't until 1988 that President Reagan signed into law the Civil Liberties Act whereby the U.S. government officially acknowledged the injustice of the internment camps and apologized for the unlawful and unjust incarceration of tens of thousands of American citizens.

James Madison issued a prescient warning: **"Of all the evils to public liberty, war is perhaps the most to be dreaded, because it comprises and develops every other."**

There are many examples throughout both recent and distant history demonstrating how eager and willing our government is to take away our freedoms in the name of security. They are quick to create or exploit war, conflict, or crisis in order to seize or expand their control over the people. They tell us that we must be willing to sacrifice our freedom and allow egregious violations of our civil liberties and privacy to keep us safe. It's for our own good, they say. And if we do not accept their abuse of our rights, they will not hesitate to use the power of the gun through law enforcement and the national security state against us.

An eerie illustration of this occurred when a Japanese American who was thrown into an internment camp during World War II asked, "If we were put there for our protection, why were the guns at the guard towers pointed inward, instead of outward?"[5]

In the fall of 2001, just six weeks after al-Qaeda Islamist terrorists launched the deadliest terrorist attack on American soil in history, Congress passed the USA Patriot Act with strong bipartisan support and very little debate. With this legislation, a bipartisan Congress completely overhauled U.S. surveillance laws, vastly expanding the government's authority to spy on everyday Americans and minimizing oversight, checks and balances that should have been in place to protect our civil liberties and prevent abuse of power.

The Fourth Amendment of the Constitution explicitly protects us from "unreasonable searches and seizures" by the government: "**The right of the people to be secure in their persons, houses, papers, and effects, against unreasonable searches and seizures, shall not be violated, and no Warrants shall issue, but upon probable cause, supported by Oath or affirmation, and particularly describing the place to be searched, and the persons or things to be seized.**"

Yet, the secret Foreign Intelligence Surveillance Act (FISA) Court that was initially created in 1978 with safeguards to protect civil liberties, saw its powers dramatically increased through the Patriot Act and those civil liberties safeguards eroded. Those enhanced powers have been used countless times to violate our Fourth Amendment rights in the darkness of a secret one-sided court. What does this look like? A rotating set of judges assigned to the FISA court meet in secret with government lawyers who seek approval to conduct surveillance, sometimes against foreign entities, sometimes against Americans. There is no requirement for the government to prove probable cause, and there are no civil liberties advocates or opposing counsel in the courtroom. The court has proven to be a dependable rubber stamp for government requests, with an approval rate of over 99 percent. In thirty-three years, the court approved 34,000 requests—and denied 11.[6]

The Patriot Act allowed for credit card numbers and bank account information to be seized via subpoena, without a warrant, expanded the government's ability to surveil our electronic communications on any platform, increased the government's wiretapping authorities, enabled secret no-notice "sneak and peak" searches, and more.

While the Bush administration and leaders in Congress from both parties sold this legislation to the American people as necessary to prevent another 9/11-style attack and to go after the terrorists who had inflicted this tragedy upon our nation—a goal shared by all—the reality is that the vast majority of powers granted by this legislation were things that the national security state had been trying for years to get enacted before the terrorist attack on 9/11, but had consistently been denied by Congress specifically because of concerns that they were unconstitutional violations of Americans' civil liberties.

Not wanting to allow the national crisis and period of mourning in the wake of the 9/11 attack to go to waste, the security agencies seized upon the moment to pass these provisions, rushing them through Congress without any real debate or examination.

Although I was not in Congress at the time, I have spoken to Ron Paul, Dennis Kucinich, and others who were there, and they told me how deeply disturbed they were by what was happening. They were angry about how this massive piece of legislation was rushed through without providing the representatives of the American people the time and space to do their job, reviewing the provisions in the Patriot Act, and determining whether they were constitutional. The pressure from the Bush administration on members of Congress was real. The administration took advantage of the legitimate fears and concerns that people had in the days and weeks following the attack, as well as of the desire that most of us had to go after and destroy those who had inflicted such terrible and tragic pain and suffering on that fateful day. The Bush administration loudly and openly threatened any member of Congress who threatened to vote no, telling them that they would be blamed and responsible for the next terrorist attack on our soil—in essence, they would have blood on their hands.

Their tactics worked, by and large.

Only one U.S. senator voted against it—a Democrat named Russ Feingold. Sixty-six members of the House of Representatives voted "no," including sixty-three Democrats and three Republicans, one of whom was Ron Paul.

My, how things have changed.

Over twenty years have gone by since the USA Patriot Act was first passed. Every few years, when provisions of the Patriot Act come up for a reauthorization vote, they are rubber-stamped and approved without any honest assessment or true debate. Those of us in Congress who dared to ask questions or oppose measures that clearly violate the civil liberties of everyday law-abiding Americans were demonized using the same kind of threats the Bush administration used in the wake of the attack on 9/11 to rush the Patriot Act through Congress. Throughout the eight years I served in Congress, I worked with colleagues on both sides of the aisle on legislation to reform the Patriot Act and repeal the most egregiously unconstitutional provisions of the law. Unfortunately, there weren't many of us who were willing to stand up for both protecting our civil liberties *and* ensuring our national security. We argued that it was our responsibility both to uphold the Constitution and to keep the American people safe. We were treated as heretics for saying this

and met with vitriolic attacks and smears from our own colleagues and
the propaganda media. They shouted at us on the House floor, delivering fiery speeches against our legislation, ominously claiming that by
opposing the rubber-stamp approval of these government surveillance
measures we would be inviting terrorists to launch another 9/11 style
attack on our own soil.

An important lesson for every American: Once we give up our
essential liberty to power-hungry politicians and bureaucrats in our
government, it is extremely difficult to get it back.

When I was first elected to Congress, I rented a small studio apartment a couple blocks from the U.S. Capitol. It used to be the carriage
house for dorms built in 1900 for single women working in D.C. It was
convenient for me to walk to and from my office and to the Capitol for
votes, which were sometimes called at odd hours of the night. My day
normally started at about 5:00 with morning prayer and meditation
followed by a workout in the gym or a run on the National Mall. But
one morning as I quickly scanned the news headlines before head-
ing out the door, the words on my phone jumped out at me: "NSA
COLLECTING PHONE RECORDS OF MILLIONS OF VERIZON
CUSTOMERS DAILY."[7] If I hadn't been fully awake before, I was now.
I started reading the article, and the more I read, the angrier I got. I was
a Verizon customer at the time, but it turned out the NSA was doing
this with all major cell phone carriers. How was this legal, I wondered?
It wasn't, really.

The fact that this was happening under the Obama administration was deeply disappointing. So many of us had supported Barack
Obama's presidential bid in 2008 because as a senator he had been
very outspoken in condemning the Patriot Act. He spoke on the Senate
floor in strong opposition to it because it gave license to government
officials to surveil everyday Americans without a warrant. He espoused

my view that the American people should not have to choose between individual liberty and national security. We expected that, as president, Obama would maintain his position, use the power of the presidency to end the rubber-stamp reauthorizations of the Patriot Act and bring about real change to protect our civil liberties. Unfortunately, he didn't do any of that.

When Edward Snowden leaked information to the public revealing the NSA's mass surveillance of Americans, President Obama did not take action to end this illegal warrantless search program—his first reaction was to defend the NSA's program. While, months later, after facing pressure from his supporters and civil liberties advocates in Congress, he delivered a speech promising to increase restrictions on the NSA, he was deliberately vague in his remarks, which had no meaningful impact on privacy protections. Seeing him so quickly go back on his commitment to protect civil liberties let down so many of us who had believed that he would keep his word.

But it wasn't just President Obama who let us down. Republican and Democrat hawks in Congress supported the Obama administration's decision to defend the NSA, citing "terrorist threats" and accusing the program's critics for not understanding the situation. They supported the NSA's continued exploitation of the vaguely worded Section 215 of the Patriot Act, which allows the government to get a secret court order that no one is allowed to see and use it to access any of our electronic records that they deem relevant to national security interests. That is a very low bar when the government is the sole authority on deciding arbitrarily how "national security interest" is defined.

A few months before Edward Snowden released evidence of the government's mass surveillance, the director of national intelligence, James Clapper, was questioned under oath during a public hearing about whether the Obama administration was collecting "any type of data at all on millions or hundreds of millions of Americans."

Clapper responded immediately, saying, "No, sir. . . . Not wittingly."[8]

Clapper was lying. He knew very well that for months the NSA had been forcing every telecommunications provider to turn over hundreds of millions of records of every text or phone call made on their domestic networks. Years after he lied to Congress, when evidence was revealed showing that the NSA was in fact illegally conducting mass collections of Americans' data, Clapper said that he hadn't lied under oath; he was just confused about the question and didn't understand it. He lied again, to cover up his original lie.

I was astonished by how quickly Clapper dismissed his original lie, and how easily he got away with it. Under federal law (18 U.S.C. Section 1001), knowingly and willingly concealing something from or making a false statement to Congress is a crime punishable by up to five years in prison. James Clapper was asked a simple, clear, and concise question. Clapper lied because he knew the NSA was breaking the law, spying on Americans, and they didn't want to get caught. As a permanent fixture of the cabal of warmongers in permanent Washington, he probably also knew that he could get away with it. And he did. He walked away unscathed, never charged with any crime, never held accountable. Now, he works as a national security analyst for CNN.

Meanwhile, Michael Cohen, former president Trump's longtime attorney, was charged and prosecuted for lying to Congress about the timeline of the Trump Organization plans to build a Trump Tower in Moscow, among other federal crimes. He was sentenced to serve three years in prison.

The National Security State

Historically, the Democrat Party has been skeptical of the national security state, and rightly so. Many of these agencies have a long track record, almost since their creation, of abusing their power and acting with impunity.

As the director of the FBI, J. Edgar Hoover conducted many illegal operations—including "black bag jobs," which involved staging break-ins and planting listening devices on American citizens to gather information on people that he or the presidents he worked for didn't like. He found ways to "help" presidents he was close to, like President Johnson, by digging up dirt on their political opponents. When Hoover had limited access to President Kennedy because of Attorney General Bobby Kennedy, Hoover collected information about President Kennedy's extramarital affairs as leverage against the president. Hoover felt free to abuse his power because he knew there was no one who would hold him accountable. There was no one to stop him from using the FBI to harass, surveil, and threaten Martin Luther King Jr., a man the FBI saw as a radical who needed to be stopped at all costs.

While the CIA was first created as an organization that would simply collect information and intelligence from around the world, analyze it, and relay it to the president, the leaders of the organization and the politicians who directed them went far beyond that original mandate, conducting paramilitary operations and orchestrating coups on foreign soil. To name a few: There was the disastrous Bay of Pigs invasion, which resulted in the deaths of more than a hundred Cuban exiles who'd been deputized by the CIA to fight against Castro. The disastrous Iranian coup overthrowing Prime Minister Mossadegh in 1953, which ultimately led to the 1979 Islamic Revolution and the creation of the theocratic Islamic Republic of Iran, which laid the groundwork for the perilous nuclear standoff we face today. There's the false narrative that made it look like Saddam Hussein had weapons of mass destruction in Iraq in 2003 to justify George W. Bush and Dick Cheney's regime-change war, and more recently their failed "intelligence" reports that Russia's invasion of Ukraine in February 2022 would result in the fall of Kyiv within a week. As of February 2024, this war rages on and Kyiv still stands.

Our nation's Founders charged Congress with the responsibility of exercising oversight over the executive branch for a reason—to serve as a check that would ensure the executive branch does not abuse their power. It is Congress's job to oversee the federal agencies, scrutinize how they're spending taxpayer dollars, and ensure they are acting within the law and the Constitution.

There was a time when the Democrat Party took this responsibility seriously. Senator Frank Church led the now-famous "Church Committee" in the mid-1970s to determine "the extent, if any, to which illegal, improper, or unethical activities were engaged in by any agency of the Federal Government."[9] The committee launched a sweeping investigation into abuses by the FBI, CIA, and NSA. Their efforts led to the exposure of numerous clandestine operations and resulted in transformative changes in the oversight and operation of the U.S. intelligence community. The hope was that the Church Committee's revelations would mark a turning point in our nation's history, that there would be an end to the abuse of power and undermining of our civil liberties by the national security state. The hope was that these agencies would recommit themselves to fulfilling their mandate and ensuring the safety, security, and freedom of the American people and our country.

But that didn't happen. Instead, they have been acting as foxes guarding the henhouse—foxes that are so dangerous even our elected officials are afraid to cross them lest they themselves get chewed up.

In 2017, President Trump questioned the credibility of the FBI as they were "investigating" him based on accusations of Russian collusion that they already knew were false. In response, Senator Chuck Schumer stated in an interview that President Trump was "being really dumb" for daring to go against the intelligence community.

"Let me tell you," Schumer said, "you take on the intelligence community, they have six ways from Sunday at getting back at you. So even for a practical, supposedly hard-nosed businessman, he's being really dumb to do this."

Schumer went on to say that intelligence officials are "very upset with how [Trump] has treated them and talked about them."[10]

I was stunned. I was not at all naive about the power of the national security state. This admission, however, from one of the most high-ranking, powerful Democrats in the country accepted as normal the fact that we are not the free democratic republic we are supposed to be. He was admitting that our democracy is a charade and that our elected leaders, who have been charged with the critical task of overseeing the national security state, are too afraid to do so. Senator Chuck Schumer sent a chilling message to everyone in the country that day: the intelligence community and national security state are so supremely powerful and accountable to no one that even the president of the United States better not dare criticize them.

The national security state and its warmongering friends have many ways of retaliating against their opponents. One of the tools they often use for politically motivated attacks is the Espionage Act. It has been used primarily against political opponents—everyone from Daniel Ellsberg, who released the Pentagon Papers during the Vietnam War to, most recently, former president Donald Trump.

During my campaign for the presidency in 2020, I got a message one day out of the blue, that Daniel Ellsberg, one of America's most well-known and historic whistleblowers, wanted to meet with me during my next visit to San Francisco. He was a longtime advocate for peace and freedom of the press who spent decades sounding the alarm on the dire consequences of nuclear war, and I looked forward to meeting him. I was inspired by how willing he had been to put his own life and freedom at risk to expose the truth and hold the most powerful people in America accountable.

Ellsberg couldn't travel much at that point, due to his advanced age and health condition, so we met at his house—a humble home at the end of a long pathway tucked in a quiet grove of trees. His wife greeted me at the door with a warm hug and led me to where Daniel was seated in his library. His eyes lit up, and his voice boomed with a warm welcome, giving me a big hug as though we were longtime friends. I felt the same way—we were kindred spirits who had been fighting in the proverbial trenches carrying the torch for peace and freedom of speech and, in our own very different ways, experiencing the wrath of the government as a result.

I had seen the movie *The Post*, about Ellsberg's release of the Pentagon Papers, and read so much about his experience. I was familiar with how after he was embedded with U.S. troops in Vietnam in 1966, he realized how hopeless the war really was. Privately, Secretary of Defense Robert McNamara shared that view, but McNamara continued to justify the war publicly. Angered by this hypocrisy and the blatant lies to the American people, Ellsberg, who worked for a think tank called the RAND Corporation, released highly classified documents that revealed the government's lies by exposing the truth about what was really going on in Vietnam.

President Nixon was furious. According to the Nixon Oval Office tapes, H. R. Haldeman explained the consequences of what Ellsberg had done:

"To the ordinary guy, all this is a bunch of gobbledygook. But out of the gobbledygook comes a very clear thing. . . . You can't trust the government; you can't believe what they say; and you can't rely on their judgment; and the—the implicit infallibility of presidents, which has been an accepted thing in America, is badly hurt by this, because It shows that people do things the president wants to do even though it's wrong, and the president can be wrong."[11]

Nixon told his team to go after Ellsberg, and the "White House Plumbers" were created—the same team that would later execute the Watergate burglaries. They planned to create a scandal challenging Ellsberg's mental state of mind by stealing his health records, and they conducted illegal wiretapping without a court order to gather evidence against him.

President Nixon and his team were not messing around. Daniel Ellsberg was accused of violating the Espionage Act of 1917, along with theft and conspiracy charges. He faced 115 years in prison. The Nixon administration was throwing everything they possibly could at him to send a message to anyone else that they dare not challenge the power of the government.

When Ellsberg turned himself in to the U.S. Attorney in Boston, he said, "I felt that as an American citizen, as a responsible citizen, I could no longer cooperate in concealing this information from the American public. I did this clearly at my own jeopardy and I am prepared to answer to all the consequences of this decision."[12]

Then he went to work to prepare his defense.

The trial began on January 3, 1973. Dan explained to me that the crux of his defense argument was that the documents he released were illegally classified—that they weren't classified to protect national security secrets from the enemy, but rather to keep secrets from the American people. The government did not want the American people to know the truth, so they classified the documents, knowing that if anyone did what Ellsberg would eventually do and release them to the public, they would be charged with a crime.

The problem for Ellsberg was that he was never allowed to make this argument in court. The judge silenced him. Why? Because the Espionage Act explicitly prohibits the defendant from explaining his or her motive to the jury. Ellsberg could not defend himself because he was not allowed to tell the judge and the jury *why* he did what did—that he had released the documents to serve a greater public interest—transparency, peace, and freedom of speech.

This rule built into the Espionage Act violates the very foundation of our justice system—that one is innocent until proven guilty, and that every American has the right to defend ourselves in a court of law.

Ellsberg's case was eventually thrown out because of the government's illegal wiretapping and misconduct, but he felt so strongly about challenging the unconstitutional nature of the Espionage Act that at ninety years old, he handed a *New York Times* reporter a top secret document he had held on to for decades. Ellsburg was prepared to go to prison to have the fight in court he never had the opportunity to have fifty years earlier—to challenge the constitutionality of the Espionage Act because, as he explained, "The question—which hardly anyone realizes, I would say, is a question—is whether this application of the Espionage Act to people who are informing the U.S. public, not secretly informing a foreign power like a spy, is constitutional."[13]

This was insanity. When we met, I was still a member of Congress, and during my visit, I promised Dan I would introduce legislation in Congress to fix this. It was not just righting a historical wrong. Espionage Act charges and prosecutions were—and still are today—being used as a political weapon against political enemies. Both Democrats and Republicans have used this, but no one more than President Obama. During his eight years in office, his administration prosecuted more people under the Espionage Act than all previous administrations combined—not for being spies or conducting espionage, but for leaking sensitive, and often embarrassing, information the government did not want the public to know about. None of them had a right to share with the court and the public why they did what they did, and therefore could not mount a proper defense.

In their fervor to punish anyone who had shared information President Obama didn't want seen by the public, the Obama administration executed unprecedented seizures of confidential files and records from journalists and news media agencies, including the personal phone records and emails of journalists. At the time, the *New York Times* editorial board stated, "The Obama administration has moved beyond protecting government secrets to threatening fundamental freedoms of the press to gather news."[14]

Even the *New York Times* recognized that though these things were done in the name of national security, that was really just a cover to go after political opponents who dared to share the truth and hold the Obama administration accountable.

President Biden and his administration have maintained the status quo, continuing this long history of abuse of power. They have sought to extradite Julian Assange to face Espionage Act charges in an American courtroom. And, in a brazen act reminiscent more of a banana republic than a democracy, the Biden administration has set their sights on former president Donald Trump, charging him with 31 violations of the Espionage Act, each carrying a possible 10-year sentence—up to 310 years in prison.[15]

On September 30, 2020, I kept my promise to Daniel Ellsberg and introduced HR 8452, the Protect Brave Whistleblowers Act of 2020, which expands whistleblower protections and allows Americans to defend themselves in court, specifically including a public interest defense. However, the political elite in Washington were not and are not interested in fixing this problem and refused to move the bill forward for a hearing and a vote. The Democrat elite want to continue keep this as a weapon in their political arsenal, targeting opponents like Donald Trump, ensuring they are refused their most basic right of defending themselves in a court of law.

Government-Controlled Currency

The Biden administration and the Democrat elite are looking for every opportunity to extend the long arm of government into controlling every aspect of our lives they can get their hands on. One of the most concerning is their desire to control our money through a central bank digital currency (CBDC). Consider a "comprehensive" fact sheet on a "First-Ever Comprehensive Framework for Responsible Development of Digital Assets" released in September 2022. This report advocates for the creation of a "U.S. CBDC—a digital form of the U.S. dollar" citing its' "potential to offer significant benefits." The report goes on to list the many "benefits" that could come from the implementation of a government-controlled digital dollar. Naturally, all these benefits sound great on the surface. But it's what they're not telling us that should concern you, because we've heard this line before. No matter how many flowery words they use to convince us that switching to a CBDC would be for our own good, or how many times they deny any ulterior motive for developing this central digital currency, we know the truth: this is about control. They want total control. They want the power to surveil and control every aspect of our lives. While they say that the same privacy laws that apply to our bank accounts would apply here, the reality is a digital currency that is centrally controlled by the government means giving up our control and our privacy.

Ultimately, a central bank digital currency will give them the power to control how we spend our money. They could prevent us from purchasing certain items and enable them to freeze our accounts—something they can't do with the cash in our wallets. Imagine this scenario: the president declares a national emergency, announces a supply shortage of a necessary product, then his administration takes it upon themselves, for the public good, to limit what we are allowed to purchase by quantity or to stop us from purchasing a certain item altogether. They would justify their actions on the grounds of the national emergency, which authorizes the president to do whatever he deems necessary—including control our money.

This is a very plausible scenario that we've already seen occur with our neighbors to the north. In February 2022, Canada's prime minister, Justin Trudeau, announced that he would invoke the Emergencies Act to crack down on the truckers who were protesting Canada's draconian COVID-19 vaccine mandates. Deputy Prime Minister Chrystia Freeland said at a press conference that under this emergency order, banks would have the power to freeze the personal bank accounts of the truckers involved in the peaceful protest, without any court order or due process. She went on to say that they could also suspend the truckers' vehicle insurance.[16] In addition, the Canadian government was working to expand its "Terrorist Financing" laws to acquire the power to also freeze cryptocurrency transactions and crowdfunding platforms, to stop support of any kind from being delivered to the truckers.

Here in the United States, we've seen efforts by people like Elizabeth Warren and other Democrat senators urging credit card companies to flag and report any purchases of firearms or ammunition to "help law enforcement prevent some mass shootings by identifying suspicious gun purchases."[17] While we all would like to prevent mass shootings, these measures place the lawful acts of purchasing and owning firearms and ammunition, which are protected under the Second Amendment, in the same category of suspicion as terrorists and violent criminals. What this means is, they promise that our financial transactions are private, until they decide they're not. We already know that many of the Democrat elite would like to ditch the Second Amendment and ban firearms altogether. It's not a stretch of imagination to guess that under a central bank digital currency the government could prohibit us from purchasing anything they deemed unacceptable, like firearms and ammunition.

As we speak, legislation is quietly being pushed through, state by state, that would support the implementation of a central bank digital currency. Legislators are being told that this is merely a procedural necessity to ensure electronic financial transactions are efficient. What they're often not being told is that this legislation is a necessary precursor for the federal government to implement a CBDC in the United States.

We can see what is to come in America with the restriction and elimination of cash by what is already occurring in Europe. Christine Lagarde, the head of the European Central Bank, has spoken about a 1000-Euro cash limit for transactions. If you exceed this amount, she says, "You are on the gray market. You take your risk. If you get caught, you are fined or go to jail."[18] In France and Italy, the limit for cash transactions is 1000 and 3000 Euro. Anything beyond that is seen as potentially suspicious activity that deserves investigation. They're currently trying to implement this standard across the EU.

Here is the truth and a warning: Once we give up our economic autonomy, we give up our freedom. Once someone else controls our wallet, they control our freedom. Once that freedom is lost, it is nearly impossible to get it back.

The Bottom Line

America is supposed to be the land of the free. It's what defines us. Freedom of speech, freedom of religion, and freedom of assembly are nonnegotiable American rights guaranteed to us by the Constitution.

Sadly, we are being led by the Democrat elite who act with hostility toward these core principles, seeking to undermine them at every turn in their endless pursuit for power. They take advantage of or create crises, emergencies, even wars to conduct power grabs; and they have politicized the security state to infringe on our liberties and take away our rights.

Benjamin Franklin famously said in 1755, "Those who would give up essential liberty, to purchase a little temporary safety, deserve neither liberty nor safety."[19]

We saw it during World War II with the Japanese internment camps. We saw it after the terrorist attack on 9/11 with the Patriot Act. We saw it with COVID-19. Warmongers in Washington are amping up new wars—both cold and hot—as we speak. If we continue down this path, we will hear the familiar refrains from these neocons and warmongers about how we, the people, must be willing to sacrifice our liberty to support their power grab thinly veiled in the name of security.

We must look to our nation's history and learn from the past. Those who wake up every day driven by a selfish desire for power don't care about the truth, and they have no use for the Constitution. In fact, they see it as an obstacle standing in their way that must be undermined, overcome, or cast aside.

No matter how many empty promises or platitudes are thrown our way, we need to be vigilant and clear-eyed in understanding that their actions are an expression of their disdain for us, our freedom, for the rule of law, and for our civil liberties. It is because of that disdain that we must stand together as proud Americans to stop them from destroying the country we love.

CHAPTER THREE

No Free Speech

Rejecting the mandate in the First Amendment, the Democrat elite are undermining our right to free speech, censoring and smearing any who dare challenge their authority and power.

O ne of the things that drew me to join the Democrat Party when I was twenty-one years old was the fact that at the time they seemed to be the most reliable and passionate defenders of free speech. In Hawaii, I saw a political party that represented the big tent, welcoming people of diverse backgrounds and ideas, and encouraging robust discussion and debate. Nationally, the Democrats seemed to be willing to take courageous stands for free speech and civil liberties, even for speech that might not be popular.

Sadly, that's not the case anymore. In their obsessive pursuit of power, today's Democrat elite are only interested in protecting speech they approve of while actively trying to silence speech they don't like.

Who Could Be Against Free Speech?

I never imagined that freedom of speech would be anything but a central and uniquely American right that we could all agree must be protected regardless of political affiliation or belief. It seemed like common sense to me that once the free speech of one group or individual is taken away, then anyone's right to free speech could be taken away. If censorship becomes the norm, then who gets censored is up to whoever happens to be in power at any given time. No one is safe. Even as a kid growing up, I understood how dangerous this would be. I had read books and heard stories about oppressive authoritarian dictators and the lack of freedom people in some countries suffered. I always felt grateful that I grew up in a country that celebrated freedom, so much so that our nation's Founders enshrined our right to free speech in the Constitution. They recognized that the hallmark of any democratic republic requires a vibrant marketplace of ideas where freedom of speech and expression can thrive. They wanted to be sure that no matter which political faction or person was in power, they would be committed to upholding the Constitution, vowing to be defenders of our individual rights and freedoms.

After Islamist jihadists launched an insidious attack against our country on 9/11, I decided to enlist in the Army, swearing an oath to support and defend the Constitution of the United States against all enemies foreign and domestic. Through this experience, I came to truly understand in a very visceral way the power of the quote, **"I may disagree with what you say, but I will defend to the death your right to say it."** This is not just a poetic platitude. Those words couldn't be more real to me and my brothers and sisters in uniform who take our oath to heart and are willing to lay down our lives to protect and defend the freedoms of all Americans.

Unfortunately, fewer and fewer Democrats agree with this sentiment. Democrats such as Representative Stacey Plaskett say that "free speech is not absolute."[1] That's a frightening new norm that today's Democrat elite have adopted. Given how little our elected officials value our Constitutional right to free speech, we should not be surprised to see an entire generation of young Americans are not being taught civics or about what our Founders intended when they crafted and signed the Constitution and Bill of Rights. Instead, they are being taught that "hate speech" is violence and that "disinformation" must be banned, without confronting the most important question: who gets to decide what speech is hate speech and what information is disinformation? They are told to seek out "safe spaces" where they will never hear anything that could offend them. Knowing this, it's understandable why there are a growing number of people who conclude that our Constitution and the First Amendment are irrelevant or, worse, pose a risk to their well-being.

This shift in our society is leading us to a dangerous place—where our thriving marketplace of ideas is being reduced to a silenced town square permeated with fear. More and more people feel they must self-censor rather than risk retaliation or ridicule.

While America is not alone in including a right to free speech in its Constitution, it is not as common as one might think. The right to speak freely doesn't exist in places like Iran and North Korea, where you can be killed for saying anything critical of the country's leaders. But even in Western countries like Australia and the United Kingdom, surprisingly, free speech is not a guaranteed right protected by their Constitution. I was shocked to hear that shortly after Prince Harry and his family moved to the United States, he said, "I've got so much I want to say about the First Amendment as I sort of understand it, but it is bonkers."[2] Free speech is bonkers?! What's bonkers is that back in Harry's home country, the British Crown Prosecution Service had to backtrack after it argued that parts of the Bible "are simply no longer appropriate in modern society and . . . would be deemed offensive if stated in public."[3]

In the United States of America, the oldest democracy in the world, we can and should serve as a living example of what a free society can be, with a vibrant marketplace of ideas where people from all backgrounds and views can speak freely without fear of retaliation from the power elite in government, Big Tech, and the propaganda media.

This free society is what our Founders envisioned for America, and what they hoped we would achieve in our journey toward being "a more perfect union." Unfortunately, we are a long way off from achieving that goal. The Democrat elite in power are doing all they can to stop us from getting there.

In July 2023, the House Select Committee on the Weaponization of the Federal Government held a hearing focused on the federal government's role in censoring Americans directly and indirectly through collusion with Big Tech.

The lead witness for this hearing was Robert F. Kennedy Jr., one of the plaintiffs in the lawsuit *Missouri v. Biden*—a free speech suit which alleges the Biden administration has directly undermined and interfered with Americans' First Amendment right to free speech.

Robert Kennedy Jr. sat in the witness seat and started getting ready to deliver his opening statement about the *Missouri v. Biden* lawsuit and why the judge's injunction prohibiting the federal government from coordinating or colluding with social media companies to censor speech was so significant.

But before Kennedy could begin his testimony, a member of the committee turned on her microphone and requested to be recognized.

Chairman Jim Jordan recognized former Democratic National Committee Chairwoman Representative Debbie Wasserman Schultz, who went on to introduce a motion on behalf of the Democrats on the committee, saying, "We respectfully request that you rescind Mr. Kennedy's invitation to be here." She justified her request to censor Kennedy by wrongly accusing him of being anti-Asian and anti-Semitic. When Kennedy tried to respond to her serious and damning accusations, she would not allow him to speak, saying, "I reclaim my time."[4]

As I watched the hearing play out on CSPAN, I was stunned by the absurdity and irony of it all. The Democrats were trying to silence Kennedy, who was there as a witness invited by the committee, in a hearing about the danger of the government taking away American's right to free speech.

Rep. Wasserman Schultz's motion was called for a vote, and the clerk began to call the roll. As she called each name, the camera panned from one Democrat to the next. During these votes, the response is very straightforward: Yea or Nay. Instead of responding in this way, my former Democrat colleagues made snide comments or remarks about why they believed Robert F. Kennedy Jr. was not entitled to free speech and should not be heard. They criticized Republicans for platforming Kennedy's "hateful, evidence-free rhetoric." The head Democrat on the Committee, ranking member Stacey Plaskett, said about Republicans, "They intentionally chose to elevate this rhetoric to give these harmful, dangerous views a platform in the halls of the United States Congress. That's endorsing that speech. That's not just supporting free speech. They have co-signed on idiotic bigoted messaging."[5]

Kennedy responded to the Democrats simply: "This is an attempt to censor a censorship hearing."[6]

Kennedy is just one of many targets of the censorship that has become all too frequent, whether by the government or by the woke cancel culture brigade.

Every day there are new examples. Recently, a professor at UC Berkeley urged her Twitter followers to commit a crime: steal and burn copies of Abigail Shrier's book *Irreversible Damage,* which details the harm transgenderism is doing to young girls.[7] Just as Abigail Shrier has every right to publish this book, the professor has every right to exercise her free speech to oppose it. Instead of supporting the right of all parties to exercise their free speech, however, the American Civil Liberties Union (ACLU), once a great champion of free speech, decided to pick sides. An attorney for the ACLU expressed opposition to Shrier's book and said, "Stopping the circulation of this book and these ideas is 100% a hill I will die on."[8]

Another example: a group of more than six hundred publishing industry employees signed an open letter in October 2022 calling on Penguin Random House to cancel a book deal they had signed with Supreme Court justice Amy Coney Barrett. Why? They hadn't read the book. There was no leaked draft they were objecting to. They didn't have any insight into what kind of book Justice Barrett would write. Their sole cause of opposition was her vote to overturn *Roe v. Wade.* Their reasoning? They felt publishing Barrett's book would be a violation of international human rights simply because Amy Coney Barrett does not believe abortion is a constitutional right.[9]

For that, according to these publishers and those terrified by views at odds with their own, Justice Barrett must be silenced.

The answer to hateful, reprehensible speech is not censorship. It is *more speech.* It is far better to defeat arguments than it is to censor them. More speech creates the opportunity to defeat the weakness of arguments in public, and to influence others to recognize and accept a superior argument. This is the hallmark of a functioning democratic society that defends free speech and celebrates an open marketplace of ideas.

Over the years, we've seen attacks on free speech from across the political spectrum. Today, they come primarily from Democrats, 70 percent of whom say they are "not opposed" to government censorship of speech, according to recent polling by Pew Research Center.[10] They believe there is some speech so reprehensible that it does not fall under the protection of the First Amendment. This argument, of course, isn't new—it's been made before. Those who wish to infringe upon the rights of others *always* believe they are doing so in service of a noble cause. Sometimes, that may be true. Too often, however, the speech they want to censor is merely speech they disagree with or speech that exposes the weakness of their position. In either case, censorship is the wrong answer.

The American Civil Liberties Union (ACLU) was for a long time lauded as the stalwart defenders of free speech. Unfortunately, that legacy and reputation ended abruptly in 2017 when the ACLU completely reversed their position and issued new guidelines stating that ACLU lawyers would now decide which free speech cases to take based on whether that speech contains "values that are contrary to our values," and whether it might cause "offense to marginalized groups."[11]

The timing of this 180-degree reversal of the ACLU's most essential principle was not coincidental. Donald J. Trump was elected president of the United States in 2016, against all odds and expectations. The Washington establishment was furious. Trump represented a direct threat to their power when he ran on a campaign promising to "drain the swamp." He didn't care about the Washington elite of either party, or the propaganda media, and he certainly didn't answer to them. So they vowed to do all they could to silence, smear, and destroy him, and they haven't stopped since, no matter the cost to our nation and our democracy. The ACLU decided to join the Democrat elite, propaganda media, and Big Tech in this mission. The ACLU is now a partisan organization in all but name, defending the right to free speech only for those who share their "values," which, not coincidentally, are aligned with whatever the "values" of the Democrat elite happen to be.

Like many people, I used to respect the ACLU as a courageous organization that took our Constitution seriously and was willing to defend the rights of all Americans, even when it was not convenient or popular.

That's clearly no longer the case. The ACLU's reversal of policy is just one example of how the Democrat elite do *not* want to uphold the Constitution. They do *not* support the Bill of Rights. And they do *not* support the First Amendment.

The Big Arm of Big Brother

On December 2, 2022, investigative journalist Matt Taibbi released what would be the first of multiple in-depth articles about the Twitter Files, where we saw evidence of something many of us had known all along: the Biden-Harris administration was (and is) working with the FBI and other agencies of the federal government to pressure Big Tech companies, directly and indirectly, to censor and suspend the accounts of specific individuals. Their defense for doing this is that they want to protect the American people from propagandists spreading disinformation and hate speech.

Before Elon Musk bought Twitter, now called X, the Biden administration was directing Twitter to censor or cancel different accounts by name, including those of everyday Americans, members of Congress, small business owners, veterans, journalists, and nonprofit leaders. After all I'd experienced, it didn't surprise me in the least to see my name on the list. I noticed a common thread among many names on the list—we were all in some way critical of or challenging the Biden administration's positions and actions.

Taibbi's articles provided irrefutable evidence that the U.S. government was circumventing the Constitution by directing private corporations to do the dirty work of censoring free speech. Even after this exposé, the Democrat elite in Washington did nothing. They either ignored the evidence or outright denied it was happening. I was shocked that Democrats I had worked with in Congress, people I knew as staunch supporters of free speech and who at one time even criticized President Obama's violation of our civil liberties, were now silent. In the face of the Biden administration's glaring abuse of power, they were unwilling to state the obvious: the Biden administration's attempt to silence Americans is wrong, unconstitutional, and must be stopped.

I've been sounding the alarm bells on this threat for years. I've had firsthand experience with this abuse of power, and government working with Big Tech and social media companies to undermine our free speech, democracy, and elections.

As a candidate for president in the Democratic Primary, I flew to Miami, Florida, on June 25, 2019, for what would be the first of many presidential primary debates. There were twenty candidates running at that time, too many to fit on one debate stage, so the organizers drew names from a hat and split the group in half. Ten of us would be on the stage each night; my name was pulled to kick off the first night of the debate.

Unlike many politicians, my experience participating in debates was limited to my run for Congress. As a very introverted kid, I relied on my extroverted younger sister to be my spokeswoman whenever we needed to interact with someone I didn't know. I was quite happy to bury my nose in books, go surfing, and limit my interactions with strangers to a bare minimum. At that time, the mere thought of speaking in front of a group of people made me sick to my stomach.

As the first debate loomed, I made sure to prepare. I did not take the opportunity to stand on that stage and speak to tens of millions of Americans lightly. I needed to maximize every minute I had to share my heart with the American people, and to let them know why I was offering to serve as their president and commander in chief. So I got ready. I pored through my notes, scribbling ideas in the margins of my binder. We held mock debates in our living room, setting up makeshift podiums made of used Home Depot cardboard boxes, and went back and forth with role players acting as other candidates and a moderator enforcing the time.

I arrived in Miami a day before the debate to sequester myself in a quiet room and capture some rare time of solitude, reflection, and preparation. Not many people in the country knew my name or had ever heard of me, not to speak of knowing that I was running for president, and why. My hope was that if the debate went well, I could effectively introduce myself to the American people so that they might be interested to learn more about me and my candidacy. At a minimum, I wanted to spark an interest that would cause them to go from the television to their phone or computer, and type, "Who is Tulsi Gabbard" into their Google search window.

As I focused on debate prep, my small but energetic campaign team was huddled in an apartment in Miami making sure our website and Google Ads account was ready, so when people searched for me online, the first thing they would see is a link to my website. This was a big moment for the campaign. There was no way I was going to rely on Google algorithms to decide what wacky smear attack article they wanted to push to the top of page one of the search results.

During that first two-hour-long debate, I had six and a half total minutes of airtime. It became clear to me very quickly who the propaganda media moderators were interested in hearing from—and it wasn't me. It was frustrating, but I made the most of every one of those minutes and seconds. When the debate ended, it turned out that I was the most searched candidate of the night—the outcome I had hoped for.

Unfortunately, I soon got a frantic message from the head of my tech team. "Our Google Ads account is suspended! We can't figure out why and we can't get ahold of anyone at Google to tell us how to fix it!" he said. This was a major problem. This was a critical time for my campaign and the window of interest was small and quickly closing. There was no way that the timing of Google's actions to suspend my Ads account without warning, explanation, or notice, was a mere coincidence. My team tried repeatedly to contact Google to find out why the account was suspended and what we needed to do to reinstate it. No response. No answer. No change. And then, after some time passed, our account was magically reinstated, again with no explanation or apology.

This hurt my campaign at a critical time. You only get one chance to introduce yourself to voters. Some anonymous person at Google recognized that and interfered with our efforts to reach voters. While this definitely had a negative impact on my campaign, I was more concerned about the greater implications: the world's biggest tech monopoly, Google, had just demonstrated that they have the power, and the will, to interfere in our democracy. Information is power. They operate in the shadows, without any transparency, and can manipulate what information voters are able to access about a candidate, thereby directly influencing the decisions voters make on who they cast their ballot for. If Google could get away with manipulating what information voters were able to see about me, a person who was at that time a sitting member of Congress running for president of the United States, then they can do it to anyone, anytime, anywhere, for any reason.

I couldn't just shrug my shoulders and let this go. So I filed a lawsuit against Google for the harm they caused my campaign by directly interfering with voters' access to my information. I wanted to send a message that such blatant abuse of power and responsibility cannot be allowed to go unchecked.

While I didn't know this at the time, Google has a documented track record of interfering in our elections. During testimony before Congress, Google executives claimed repeatedly that their company and its algorithms have no political bias. But the facts tell a very different story. Here is just one example: a study released in March 2022 by North Carolina State University found that during the 2020 presidential campaign, of the massive number of political emails sent to Gmail accounts from candidates representing both political parties, 10 percent of "left-wing" emails were sent to spam folders, while 77 percent of "right-wing" emails were sent to spam.[12]

Google decides which emails they want the voters to see, and which get diverted to spam folders where they will never see the light of day. That's a lot of power. And they're using it. Google and companies like it are actively and intentionally trying to manipulate, influence, and steal our democracy, often working hand in glove with the Democrat elite.

Regardless of your political affiliation or which candidate you like or dislike, here's why you should be concerned: If this Big Tech monopoly, with the backing of a highly politicized national security state, has the power to control what we see and don't see, and censor what we are allowed to say, then we, as voters, are no longer free to gather the information we need to make our own decisions about who we want to vote for—or to exercise our own freedom of speech.

We are left with information that is so curated that we only see the candidates and information that the Washington permanent elite want us to see.

This is not America. Without freedom of speech, expression, and the ability to make informed decisions for ourselves, our democracy is doomed.

My lawsuit against Google was dismissed by U.S. District Judge Stephen Wilson, who said that I failed to establish "how Google's regulation of its own platform is in any way equivalent to a governmental regulation of an election. Google does not hold primaries, it does not select candidates, and it does not prevent anyone from running for office or voting in elections. To the extent Google 'regulates' anything, it regulates its own private speech and platform."

Judge Wilson missed the point. His statement is based on a reality that doesn't exist in our country today. He ignored the proven collaboration that exists between our government and Big Tech. While Google and the other Big Tech giants are not government entities, under the Biden-Harris administration, they are acting as a de facto arm of the Democrat elite. They work to support the interests of the Democrat elite by manipulating and limiting what information voters can access, silencing those the Democrat elite don't want heard—and they do it all in the name of suppressing "hate speech" or "disinformation."

Why are they so intent on controlling what we say and what we see? They know that if they stopped meddling with our democracy and undermining our free speech, the American people would learn the truth about them—they don't care about us or the Constitution. They are more interested in serving their own self-interests and feeding their insatiable greed for power. By allowing a truly free society where we can think and speak for ourselves, they would risk being directly challenged by those who have the ability to take their power away— "We, the people."

On March 9, 2023, members of Congress gathered on the floor of the House of Representatives to cast their vote on the Protecting Speech from Government Interference Act. This bill was introduced largely because of the information revealed in the Twitter Files and the ongoing attempts by the Biden-Harris administration to undermine free speech by directing Big Tech to censor and silence people.

You would think this bill would easily pass unanimously. Every American who values freedom should support this bill, right? Certainly, every member of Congress who swore an oath to "support and defend the Constitution of the United States" should resoundingly vote Yes. Who would dare vote against protecting free speech? Apparently, 206 Members of Congress would, and did.

As happens with every roll call vote in Congress, when the vote begins, a projector lights up the wall above the Speaker's rostrum with the names of every member of Congress. As each representative goes to cast their vote by sliding their voting card into one of the many voting machines mounted on the backs of the seats on the House floor, their vote pops up on the wall next to their name in form of a letter: Y for Yes, N for No, or P for Present.

On this day, as each vote was cast, a clear line was drawn in the sand, revealing who stands for free speech and who does not.

Of all the members of Congress voting that day, every Republican voted for the bill to protect free speech—and every Democrat voted against it.[13]

Their reason? The Democrat elite believe that the government (obviously referring to themselves) has not only the right, but the responsibility, to "protect" the American people from "disinformation."

This raises the question: Who gets to say what is disinformation or information? What objective government entity is the arbiter of truth versus fiction?

Nowhere in the Constitution or Bill of Rights does it say that we as Americans are limited to free speech and expression so long it is based on fact. Our founding documents do not state that all speech must be protected except for disinformation. The Founders did not create some authority or entity that has the unilateral power to decide who is allowed to speak and who is not, or what is deemed information versus disinformation. They did the exact opposite, choosing to enshrine in the Bill of Rights our First Amendment right protecting free speech from any attempt of a tyrannical government to censor us.

And yet in the depths of their arrogance, the Democrat elite completely reject the words and spirit of the First Amendment by appointing themselves as the sole authority and decider of who shall be censored and whose voice shall be heard.

Of course, they tell us they are doing this for our own good, to protect us from speech that may be "harmful" or could mislead us. They believe we are too stupid to think for ourselves, and that we must cede our ability to think and draw our own conclusions to them so they can tell us what we are allowed to say and see and what we must think and do.

Democrat representative Daniel Goldman of New York claimed that voting against the resolution to stop federal policing of online speech would be a way to "stand with free speech and American democracy." He feels the government must have the authority to stop Russia and China from spreading "disinformation."[14] (The irony of his believing that government censorship is a way to "stand with free speech and American democracy" is inexplicable and beyond the pale.)

What kind of disinformation is he referring to? The kind of "Russian disinformation" that fifty-one former high-level intelligence officials manufactured out of thin air to keep voters from seeing damning information on Hunter Biden's laptop that could have implicated Joe Biden just weeks before the 2020 election? Biden's campaign knew that if voters saw what was on Hunter Biden's laptop, it might cause voters to think twice before voting for Biden. Unwilling to take that risk, current secretary of state Antony Blinken, then a senior Biden campaign official, reached out to former acting CIA director Mike Morell and asked him to "help Biden" by enlisting his former colleagues in the intelligence community to sign a letter warning the American people that the Hunter Biden laptop "has all the classic earmarks of a Russian information operation."[15] There was no evidence of this, and they knew it. An IRS whistleblower reported that the FBI had confirmed in November 2019 that there was zero Russian interference with Hunter's laptop—one year before the 2020 election, and almost a year before these former senior intelligence officials released their letter.[16]

The Biden campaign was not willing to let the truth get in the way of winning the election, so they worked directly with Morell to get the letter done. The timing of this was critical—Trump was attacking Biden relentlessly on Hunter Biden's corruption, and Biden needed something he could use to shut down Trump's line of attack in an upcoming debate.

The Biden campaign leaked the letter to friendly so-called journalists who broke the story on October 19, 2020, less than thirty days before the election, with the headline, "Hunter Biden Story is Russian disinfo, dozens of former officials say."[17]

President Biden used this letter as his "evidence" a few days later during an October 22 presidential debate against Donald Trump. As planned, he immediately dismissed Trump's accusations that he and his family were profiting from peddling influence in foreign countries. Biden flippantly said it was all just "a Russian plan" and pointed to this manufactured letter by "fifty former national intelligence folks" as proof.[18]

It worked. The letter made headlines. It was repeated over and over by propaganda media. The contents of the laptop were barred from being released on Twitter. Mike Morell testified to Congress that he had gotten a call from Steve Ricchetti, then chairman of the Biden campaign, after that October debate to personally thank him for the letter.[19] They had accomplished their goal. The "disinformation" tactic was effectively used to block voters from seeing the contents of the Hunter Biden laptop before the election.

‘ The Democrat elite deprived the American people of potentially damaging information about Biden in the days and weeks leading up to the election because they were afraid that if voters saw the information, Biden might not win the election. They politicized and weaponized the national security state, worked with their partners in the propaganda media and Big Tech, and stole our democracy from right under our noses in broad daylight.

To this day, not a single person involved in this lie has apologized or been held accountable.

Shortly after the House of Representatives passed the Protecting Speech from Government Interference Act, a federal court ruled that the federal government must immediately stop any contact with social media companies for the purpose of "encouraging, pressuring, or inducing in any manner the removal, deletion, suppression, or reduction of content containing protected free speech."[20]

The Biden administration was aghast that a judge had the audacity to challenge their authority and uphold the First Amendment. Because of the ruling, the White House was forced to cancel previously scheduled meetings with Meta and Google where they had planned to discuss collaborating on how best to "counter domestic extremism" and ensure the 2024 election is free of "disinformation."

Counter domestic extremists? Like who? The so-called "MAGA Republicans" that President Biden has labeled as the greatest threat to our democracy? Or maybe it's the "radical traditional Catholics" the FBI deems a threat because they prefer traditional Latin Mass. Or perhaps it's parents who object to the overt sexualization of their young children at school. Or those standing up against the irreversible surgeries that mutilate our kids in the name of "gender-affirming care."

The Biden administration expressed in no uncertain terms that they would fight the court's ruling because allowing the court to stop them from working with Big Tech to censor Americans would cause "great harm."

I smiled and laughed a little when I read their response because of the sliver of honesty that slipped through. I agreed with the White House's response—the court banning their censorship activities would cause great harm—but not to the American people, our security, or our democracy. The ones who would experience "great harm" are the Democrat elite. Their power is threatened when we, the people, can decide for ourselves what information we read and hear, and when we exercise our right to free speech by debating and sharing our thoughts, ideas, and questions in an open marketplace of ideas that is the hallmark of a free society.

Those in power who put their own self-interest ahead of the interest of the people and our country are weak, insecure people who wake up every day afraid of losing their power and are willing to do whatever it takes to keep it.

The Bottom Line

The idea that we must blindly accept and follow what those in power tell us is true goes against the very essence of our Constitution and Bill of Rights, which were created as a resounding rejection of the reign of kings, churches, and authorities.

Instead of honoring and upholding the vision that our nation's Founders had for us as Americans to live in a free society, the Democrat elite seek to destroy any who dare challenge them.

Thomas Jefferson talked about cowardly, power-hungry leaders like these when he said they "prefer the calm of despotism to the boisterous sea of liberty."[21]

Today's "leaders" are terrified by the prospect of the American people harnessing our voices and our freedom and exposing them for the frauds they really are. They are terrified of what will happen when we, the people, exercise our intrinsic freedom to seek the truth, speak freely, and question their authority. Because they are driven by this fear, instead of a government ordained "to secure these rights," we now face a government led by the Democrat elite who are determined to take these rights away. They will stop at nothing to do so. This is not freedom or democracy. This is authoritarianism.

Harry Truman once said, "America was not built on fear. America was built on courage, imagination, and an unbeatable determination to do the job at hand."[22]

We cannot cower in fear when the foundational pillars of our country are under attack. Our future, and that of this country that we love, is in our hands. We have been given a must-not-fail mission by none other than the Founders of this great nation. They were talking about us when they said "We, the people." They were talking about us when they spoke of a "self-government."

We may not agree on every issue; neither did our Founding Fathers. They debated and argued fiercely, yet they stood together on what mattered most: love of country, respect and love for one another as children of God, and an unwavering commitment to upholding the Constitution and our God-given rights and freedoms.

We must be clear-eyed about what is at stake in this moment. If we are to have any hope of saving our country, we must take action. Staying on the sidelines or remaining silent is not an option. We must speak up, stand firm, and stop those undermining our freedom from destroying our country and extinguishing the light of freedom that has burned brightly for so long.

CHAPTER FOUR

They See God as the Enemy

Those in control of today's Democrat Party are actively under-mining our religious freedom, trying to erase the presence of God from every facet of public life, and are openly hostile toward people of faith and spirituality.

Freedom of religion is often called the first of our freedoms. The opening line of the First Amendment to the Constitution reads, "Congress shall make no law respecting an establishment of religion or prohibiting the free exercise thereof."

Our nation has deep roots in the foundation of religious liberty, and our founding documents reflect the great care our Founders took to protect the rights of people to worship as they see fit, or not to worship at all, and to defend that freedom of expression for every American from persecution or oppression by the state.

I cannot associate myself with today's Democrat Party, the leaders of which stand in direct opposition to this freedom, intent on using all the levers of their power to target people of faith, especially Christians, and undermine our religious freedom.

I am forever grateful to my parents for many things in my life, but I am most thankful for being raised in a home where God was the center of our everyday lives. I realized early on that I am a child of God, this material world is not my real home, and my time here is short. I was always happiest when I was trying in some way to be pleasing to God. That spiritual foundation and understanding gave me a very clear sense of purpose from a young age. I knew that what I wanted to do with my life was serve the Supreme Friend.

Some of my favorite verses from scripture that speak to this foundational truth are 2 Corinthians 5:6 and 8.

> Therefore we are always confident and know that as long as we are at home in the body we are away from the Lord.

> We are confident, I say, and would prefer to be away from the body and at home with the Lord. So we make it our goal to please him, whether we are at home in the body or away from it.

In our always lively and loud household of five rambunctious kids, and many stray passersby who always seemed to find their way to my parents' welcoming doorstep, our daily lives were grounded in a very strong spiritual foundation. Some of my earliest memories are of starting our day with morning prayers and ending it with Mom reading bedtime stories to us from the New Testament or the Bhagavad Gita, which means Song of God, the ancient Hindu scripture spoken over five thousand years ago. Before she tucked us in and gave us a kiss good-night, we would say the Lord's Prayer together. Our house was often filled with bright colors, beautiful sounds, and the fragrant aromas of Christian and Hindu celebrations.

As you might imagine, with this upbringing I had no concept of sectarianism. I never felt like I had to "choose" one religion or another. From my perspective, there is and always will be only one all-powerful, supreme, all-knowing, loving God with countless names that describe His innumerable glorious transcendental qualities and characteristics. From my childhood, I loved hearing the different names of God and including them in our morning family worship—my dad singing as he strummed his guitar, me playing the conga drums, and my sister or one of my brothers on keyboard.

In short, my religion was and is simple: loving God with all my heart and loving and caring for others as much as I love and care for myself.

During the best of times and the darkest of days in my life—while deployed to a war zone being confronted with death, destruction, and suffering; when surrounded on all sides by the most toxic, corrupt self-serving politicians; and when dealing with the pain of loss and heartbreak—my spiritual foundation and relationship with God has been my guiding light, inspiration, strength, and home. I know that no matter what's happening in my life or the world, I can always find peace and shelter in the warm embrace of God's unconditional love.

When I first joined the Democrat Party in 2002, it seemed to be an inclusive party that understood and appreciated the importance of upholding religious liberty, free expression, and welcoming people of different religions, beliefs, and views.

Unfortunately, the Democrat Party has abandoned that legacy. Party leaders believe that God has no place in our public life, and that believing in and worshipping God or expressing and celebrating love for God in public is somehow synonymous with fascism or right-wing politics.

Every couple years as we draw closer to Election Day, it's all too common to see Democrat politicians standing at the pulpit of a church on Sunday morning, quoting Bible verses and throwing out a few "Amens!" But for many, it's just lip service, and a gross attempt to exploit people's faith in God to further their own self-serving political ambitions. We can see who is phony and who is sincere through their actions. They pretend to respect people of faith to garner the support of powerful voting blocs like Blacks, Hispanics, and voters in the South or Midwest. But in reality, they condescendingly look upon people of faith as uneducated and backward. They will throw their hands up and say, "Amen!" at church so everyone hears them, but behind closed doors they show their true feelings, belittling people of faith. Barack Obama's 2008 statement (at a private fundraiser, of course) that white working-class voters in the middle of the country tend to "cling to guns or religion" is emblematic of this disrespect.[1]

I first experienced this offensive hypocrisy on the eve of my first deployment to Iraq in 2004 with Hawaii's 29th Brigade Combat Team. My dad was a city council member at the time and was running for Congress as a Republican, challenging a first-term Democrat incumbent named Ed Case. Instead of debating my dad on the issues, Case published a lengthy open letter to my dad, aiming to foment religious bigotry by demanding that my dad answer many offensive questions about his religion, beliefs, and practices. His intent was obvious; he was trying to raise suspicion in voters' minds that my dad was a liar who couldn't be trusted, directly accusing my dad of not being a "real Catholic."

That pissed me off.

I had sworn an oath to support and defend the Constitution of the United States, which guarantees our God-given rights and freedoms, foremost among them the freedom every one of us has to love and worship God as we choose, or not at all. I was days away from leaving home to deploy to a war zone in the Middle East, where most countries were ruled by theocracies that sent the "religious police" to hunt down those who dared to defy sharia. The people in these countries had no concept of religious freedom. It simply did not exist in those places.

But here was a Congressman who had taken the same oath to the Constitution that I had—who knew that the Constitution mandates that there shall be "no religious test" for anyone wishing to serve in public office—weaponizing my dad's faith and personal relationship with God to advance his own self-serving political ambitions. Win at all costs, was his mentality.

Despicable.

Months later, while we were deployed, I was surprised when Congressman Case showed up at our camp in Iraq for a quick visit and photo op with Hawaii soldiers. My commander, knowing my background working in politics, told me that I could take some time off to go and see Case. Inside, my stomach turned. "No thank you," I told him. I had no interest in being used as a prop in his next campaign brochure.

I thought local Democrats in Hawaii would recognize how dangerous this mentality was and be angered, as I was. I thought journalists would recognize that a sitting member of Congress with such blatant disregard for the Constitution couldn't be trusted and must be exposed.

But they said nothing. The Democrat Party, influential Democrat leaders of minority religions, and the Hawaii news media not only let him off the hook, in many cases they amplified his bigoted attacks.

That happened twenty years ago. The same utter contempt for the Constitution and people of faith that Case displayed then, has now become common among many Democrats, and dangerously even more blatant.

In President George Washington's first inaugural address in 1789, he said that it would be "peculiarly improper to omit in this first official Act, my fervent supplications to that Almighty Being who rules over the Universe, who presides in the Councils of Nations, and whose providential aids can supply every human defect."[2]

Our Founders knew that freedom *of* religion did not mean freedom *from* religion. Official meetings often began with prayers, and lawmakers often referenced God when introducing and debating legislation. For most of American history, presidential candidates of both parties made frequent reference to God both during their campaign speeches and once they were elected to office.

The U.S. Constitution prevents the establishment of a *national* religion, but it does not abolish our right to worship as we choose. The First Amendment guarantees not just freedom of religion but the free *exercise* of religion.

For a while, the religious differences between Democrats and Republicans were barely noticeable. In 1976, the United States elected president a Democrat, Jimmy Carter, a "born-again" Christian and a personal friend of the evangelical leader Reverend Billy Graham. But according to Amy Sullivan, a professor who looks at the relationship between religion and politics, Carter's White House staff considered his Christian faith to be a political liability because much of the Democrat Party leadership at that time—especially the liberal elites in New York City and Washington—had moved away from God.[3] For many of them, religion cast doubts on one's liberalism and therefore was no longer acceptable, unless it was kept private, or used selectively, only in front of certain audiences.

Throughout President Bill Clinton's eight years in the White House, the shift toward secularism and atheism among Democrats continued.

President Clinton had been raised in small-town Arkansas and could recite Bible verses with the precision of an ordained minister. But it seemed that that was deployed strategically, to win over swing voters.

In 2004, the Democrat Party's platform mentioned God seven times. By the time I ran for Congress in 2012, however, mentions of God had disappeared almost completely from the Democrat Party's platform. The Democrat Party platform for the election year 2020 mentioned God just once. Even that single mention was too much for Dr. Marisa Richmond, a delegate to the DNC, who made sure to omit the words "under God" from the Pledge of Allegiance during that convention, choosing instead to remain silent between "one nation" and "indivisible."[4]

I had a front-row seat to this when I was vice chair of the Democratic National Committee, attending various Democrat Party events and gatherings across the country. At these political conventions, speeches, and roundtables, it was uncommon to hear someone offer a prayer, or mention God or religion. You *could* do it, of course. But if you did, there was an almost palpable negative feeling in the room, with many nearly cringing at the mention of God.

This quiet at first, and then increasingly public hostility toward God, spirituality, and people of faith bothered me tremendously because of the threat this attitude poses to religious liberty.

Etched into the wall of the Jefferson Memorial in Washington, D.C. are these powerful words: "God who gave us life gave us liberty. Can the liberties of a nation be secure when we have removed a conviction that these liberties are the gift of God?"

To recognize each other as children of God, is to appreciate that we belong to God, and no one else. No government or person has the right to take away the freedom God has given us.

In the early months of the COVID-19 pandemic, Democrat leaders mandated that churches, temples, and mosques shutter their doors, while allowing major retail chains, strip clubs, casinos, and liquor stores to remain open. These were deemed "essential businesses," while places of worship were not.

In Oregon, officials allowed a church auditorium to be used for an exercise class of any size so long as attendees practiced social distancing. However, if pastors had twenty-five people congregating in that very same auditorium for church services, they were threatened with fines and jail time.

The City of Greenville, Mississippi, banned drive-in church services, and brought in the police, who issued $500 tickets to people sitting in their cars in the church parking lot listening to their pastor's sermon on the radio. Similar bans on drive-in church services were implemented in Tennessee, Michigan, and other states. In all cases, drive-in restaurants continued to operate with no harassment and threat.

Pastors who dared to defy these orders by holding regular church services were threatened, arrested, and publicly smeared, called "grandma killers" and "religious fanatics."

The entities our government chose to deem "essential," versus those they did not, reveals how screwed up their priorities are and what they really care about. They place greater value on a liquor store than a church; greater importance on a casino than a group of people gathering outside to worship. They are consumed by materialism, with no regard for the spiritual well-being of our country or our people, and their animosity toward people of faith knows no bounds.

There was clearly a double standard at play. The mainstream media and government officials did not apply the same rules across the board. The COVID-19 lockdown certainly did not apply to Black Lives Matter rioters, who gathered mobs of people, burgled local shops, and burned down police headquarters without accountability or prosecution. Even as we were told to stay at home and people of faith were prohibited from coming together to worship, public health officials encouraged hundreds of thousands of people across the country to gather and march in the wake of George Floyd's death. The same public health officials who told us we couldn't leave our homes or go to church joined these marches and urged others to do the same, saying that marching for "social justice" was more important than the public health risk posed by the COVID-19 pandemic—the same pandemic they used as an excuse to keep us in our homes and jail pastors who dared to gather with parishioners to worship.

The bias against people of faith doesn't stop there.

The Biden administration has escalated its attacks on people of faith more than any other presidency in history. The Catholic League is the nation's largest Catholic civil rights organization working to "safeguard both the religious freedom rights and the free speech rights of Catholics whenever and wherever they are threatened." Bill Donohue, an Air Force veteran and longtime civil liberties advocate who is the president of the Catholic League, said recently, "When I first started out, most of the anti-Catholicism was coming from the media, the entertainment industry, the arts, education, primarily there," he said. "It's changed. It's coming now more from the Corporate 500, from the United States government, as well as from some state and local governments."[5]

With the passage of Obamacare in 2011 came a federal mandate that all employers must provide free contraceptives, including the week-after pill. While there was a narrow religious exemption, Obama's Department of Health and Human Services determined it did not apply to religious nonprofits like the Little Sisters of the Poor, an order of nuns whose religious beliefs would make it impossible for them to comply. The Obama administration provided exemptions to their big-dollar donors at companies like Exxon, Pepsi, and Visa but refused the Little Sisters of the Poor their exemption request and maliciously threatened them with tens of millions of dollars in fines for failure to comply. In the face of this blatant abuse of power directly targeted at the Little Sisters with intent to harm them, the Little Sisters of the Poor courageously filed a lawsuit against the federal government for violating their religious freedom. The Obama administration, exposing their disgust and hate for people of faith, fought back, kicking off an extremely costly years-long battle. The nuns wouldn't budge. They continued the fight all the way to the Supreme Court, which finally ruled in favor of the right of these nuns and every American to be free to practice their faith in every aspect of their lives, upholding the principle that the government has no authority to force people to violate their religious beliefs.[6]

In a memo dated January 23, 2023, an intelligence analyst in the FBI's Richmond office authored a memo entitled "Racially or Ethnically Motivated Violent Extremists in Radical Traditionalist Catholic Ideology Almost Certainly Presents New Mitigation Opportunities." When I read this, I wondered, what are the characteristics of a "radical traditionalist Catholic?" My dad is Catholic and a lector at St Jude's in Hawaii. Was he now going to be targeted for going to Mass? Among other things, the analyst notes, "radical traditionalist Catholics" prefer to attend traditional Latin Mass. One of the recommended courses of action proposed in this memo to "mitigate[e]" this purported threat is for the FBI to develop "sources" within the church who can surveil fellow parishioners in their place of worship. The FBI disavowed this memorandum once it was leaked publicly, saying, it "does not meet the exacting standards of the FBI"—hardly a full-throated rejection of the dangerous religious bigotry and unconstitutional abuse of power within its agency.[7] The real threat this incident exposed does not come from devout Catholics—it is the threat coming from the Biden administration and agencies like the FBI who have created a culture in which it seems credible that devout people of faith, of any religion or spiritual practice, pose a threat to our country and should be targeted.

In 2019, the Trump administration implemented the Religious Liberty and Free Inquiry rule, which would withhold federal aid from any higher education institution that did not ensure religious student groups had the same First Amendment rights as other student groups. Christian student groups have been suspended or banned altogether by university administrators for not allowing students to serve in club leadership if they don't agree with the religious views of the club. This seems like common sense for any club or organization. Why should someone who hates chess be allowed to serve as the head of the chess club? Why would someone who adheres to a carnivore diet lead the plant-based vegan club? Similarly, why would an atheist be allowed to serve as head of a Christian club, or a Christian to head an atheist club?

The Biden administration does not recognize how this common-sense rule is important to protect the First Amendment right of students and is actively working to revoke the Religious Liberty rule through the Department of Education. Their excuse for revoking the rule is that it places too great a "burden" on the Department of Education and is "not necessary" because students who are discriminated against for their religious beliefs can just sue the university—placing the burden on students to have to fight the university through the courts to protect their First Amendment right.[8]

These are just a few examples of Democrat leaders' utter disregard for the Constitution and contempt toward people of faith. They are not only undermining our religious liberty, they are undermining the very foundation of our God-given rights enshrined in the Constitution. Their arrogance and hunger for power is so great that they actually believe they are an authority greater than God, and therefore can give and take away rights that come from God and threaten us at the barrel of a gun if we refuse to bend the knee to their blasphemous hubris.

No Religious Test

In 2018, President Trump nominated a prosecutor named Brian
Buescher to serve as a federal judge in Buescher's home state of Nebraska.
By all accounts, Buescher, a graduate of Georgetown University's law
school and an expert in agricultural law, was qualified for the position.
But Democrats—the self-styled "resistance"—were determined to block
everything President Trump tried to do, whether it had merit or not.
There was no chance any Democrat senator would even consider voting
to confirm Buescher, simply because he was nominated by President
Trump. Given the hyper-partisanship that had increasingly taken over
Congress, this was disheartening but not surprising. The line of attack
they chose to use in their assault to block Buescher, however, was most
reprehensible.

During her questioning of Brian Buescher before the Senate
Judiciary Committee, then senator Kamala Harris dealt what she
believed was a death blow to Buescher's nomination, talking about
Buescher's Catholic faith and his public membership in a well-known
Catholic fraternal and charitable organization as a cause for great
suspicion.

"Since 1993," she said, whispering into the microphone as if she
were uncovering and exposing a nasty bit of information in real time,
"You have been a member of the Knights of Columbus, an all-male
society comprised primarily of Catholic men."[9]

Anyone familiar with the well-used tactics of the Democrat Elite
will see exactly what Kamala Harris was doing here. By using trigger-
ing buzzwords, she was attempting to paint Buescher as some kind of
sexist, misogynistic, religious fanatic. I'm actually surprised she didn't
play the race card, too, accusing the organization of being made up of
primarily "white Catholic men," completing the Democrats' "woke"
trifecta of supposed abominations. Conveniently, she left out the fact
that John F. Kennedy had been a member of the Knights of Columbus,

that the Knights had battled for civil rights against the Ku Klux Klan, and that they are longtime supporters of the Special Olympics, among other nonprofit charity organizations.

As I listened to her line of questioning, I wondered, had she never been to Catholic Mass before, joining those she criticized in prayer? As the senator representing California, had she never been to community service events sponsored by the Knights of Columbus to provide for those in need, often in minority communities? She was wildly out of touch with reality and apparently knew nothing about the Knights of Columbus. My dad has been a longtime member of the Knights of Columbus, which in his church is predominantly made up of Filipino and Polynesian men. I've worshipped alongside them, witnessed the impact of the work they do, and seen how much time and energy they put into supporting service organizations like the Special Olympics. My aunt has been a competitor in the Special Olympics for many years, and there's nothing like seeing the huge smile on her face as she's running across the finish line, her laughter both infectious and priceless, bringing smiles to everyone cheering her and others on.

None of that mattered to Kamala Harris. Her line of questioning was purely malicious, and she was using her position as a U.S. senator to try to destroy this man because of his faith in God.

Senator Harris asked Buescher whether he was aware that the Knights of Columbus "opposed a woman's right to choose" when he joined the organization in the early 1990s. The Knights are a Catholic organization that promotes the sanctity of life and opposes abortion on religious grounds; it should not have been surprising that he knew their position.

What Kamala Harris should have known, as a senator on the Judiciary Committee, is that according to the Constitution, religious views cannot be used to disqualify anyone from a position in government; there can be no "religious test."

Like every Member of Congress, Kamala Harris swore an oath to "support and defend the Constitution of the United States against all enemies foreign and domestic; that I will bear true faith and allegiance to the same." The Constitution contains clear, concise language forbidding religious litmus tests for government service. Article VI, Clause 3, of that document reads:

> The Senators and Representatives before mentioned, and the Members of the several State Legislatures, and all executive and judicial Officers, both of the United States and of the several States, shall be bound by Oath or Affirmation, to support this Constitution; but no religious Test shall ever be required as a Qualification to any Office or public Trust under the United States.

Because of this, historically, senators have been careful, especially during televised confirmation hearings, not to explicitly demand that a candidate for a government position renounce their membership in a religious organization.

Not anymore.

Shortly after Kamala Harris concluded her line of questioning, Democrat senator Mazie Hirono from my home state of Hawaii asked Buescher directly whether he would leave the Knights of Columbus if he were confirmed as a federal judge. "The Knights of Columbus has taken a number of extreme positions," she said, drawing attention to the group's opposition to same-sex marriage. "If confirmed, do you intend to end your membership with this organization to avoid any appearance of bias?"[10]

Even though dozens of constitutional scholars pointed out that this question rose to the level of a religious litmus test, thereby violating the Constitution, no one in the Democrat Party or Senate leadership admonished Senator Hirono or Senator Harris for these violations. They were neither reprimanded nor made to answer for what they had done. Quite the contrary. The radical woke Democrats and their propaganda arms in the media celebrated and praised Hirono and Harris for their "courage," proudly touting them as leaders of the anti-Trump resistance. The message was clear: if you are a Democrat attacking white people of a predominantly "white" faith— Christianity—the most outrageous and unconstitutional forms of religious bigotry are not only acceptable but celebrated.

Senator Dianne Feinstein grilled Amy Coney Barrett in 2017, after Barrett was nominated as a judge for the Seventh Circuit Court of Appeals. During a contentious and highly politicized confirmation hearing, Senator Feinstein asked several pointed questions of Barrett, including about her weekly religious practices, her belief in Catholic doctrine, and even her adopted children. She ended her interrogation of Barrett with a shocking statement: "I think in your case, professor," she said, "when you read your speeches, the conclusion one draws is that the dogma lives loudly within you. And that's of concern when you come to big issues that large numbers of people have fought for, for years, in this country."[11]

It was not so long ago that John F. Kennedy was discriminated against because of his Catholic faith. At that point in time, the United States had never had a Catholic president, and Kennedy's opponents took advantage of that, fomenting religious bigotry by planting seeds of suspicion in voters' minds about Kennedy's loyalties, arguing that if Kennedy managed to win the White House, he would take his orders from the pope.

Kennedy directly addressed these baseless accusations with a powerful speech delivered to a group of Protestant ministers in Houston, Texas, in 1960. His words were powerful then, and just as relevant now. Kennedy said, in part,

I believe in an America that is officially neither Catholic, Protestant, nor Jewish; where no public official either requests or accepts instructions on public policy from the Pope, the National Council of Churches or any other ecclesiastical source; where no religious body seeks to impose its will directly or indirectly upon the general populace or the public acts of its officials; and where religious liberty is so indivisible that an act against one church is treated as an act against all.

For while this year it may be a Catholic against whom the finger of suspicion is pointed, in other years it has been, and may someday be again, a Jew—or a Quaker or a Unitarian or a Baptist. It was Virginia's harassment of Baptist preachers, for example, that helped lead to Jefferson's statute of religious freedom. Today I may be the victim, but tomorrow it may be you—until the whole fabric of our harmonious society is ripped at a time of great national peril.[12]

His message is clear. We must all stand up for religious freedom and against bigotry and hatred. It may not be you, your friends, family, or place of worship being targeted today. But it could be you tomorrow. An attack against one of us is an attack against all of us.

A few days after the Brian Buescher hearing, I wrote an op-ed about how the actions of these senators should outrage all Americans, regardless of their religion or politics, because of the dangerous precedent they set that threatens the core of the First Amendment: religious liberty. I wrote,

For too long in our country, politicians have weaponized religion for their own selfish gain, fomenting bigotry, fears, and suspicions based on the faith, religion or spiritual practices of their political opponents.

Whether we think of ourselves as Christians, Hindus, Muslims, Sikh, Buddhists, Jews, atheists, agnostics, or anything else, it is imperative that we stand united in our commitment to protect religious freedom and the right to worship or not worship, safely and without the fear of retribution.

Elected leaders engaging in religion-baiting are playing with fire. They are sacrificing the well-being, peace, and harmony of our country to satisfy their own political ambitions for partisan political interests.

We must stand together, call out, and reject religious bigotry no matter where it comes from, and fight to protect the freedoms and principles that bind us together as Americans.[13]

This is personal for me, not only because my father has been the target of politically motivated bigoted attacks; I've experienced it too. When I was running for Congress in 2012 and 2014, my Republican opponent stated publicly that a Hindu should not be allowed to serve in the U.S. Congress and that Hinduism is "not compatible" with the U.S. Constitution.[14] During my 2016 reelection campaign, my Republican opponent stated that, because of my religion, "A vote for Tulsi Gabbard is a vote for the devil."[15]

During my 2020 presidential campaign, there were both direct and indirect attacks on me because of my religion from the mainstream media and from so-called progressive Democrats. At one point, a major magazine was doing a lengthy profile on me and my faith, promising to be fair and unbiased. Apparently the writer was never interested in my policies, positions, or spiritual journey. He chose to dedicate the vast majority of his ink to Hinduphobic attacks, gossip, and smears coming from people who knew nothing about me, my heart, or my spiritual practice, instead of sharing the heartfelt answers I gave him about my personal relationship with God.

The taxpayer-funded National Public Radio used this same tactic against me in an interview where, during the host's introduction of me, she started off by rattling off a litany of baseless bigoted attacks, gossip, and smears she had found on the Internet about me, primarily focused on my religion. It was clear to me she had no interest in an honest conversation. It seemed that her goal was to invoke suspicion and inflict as much political damage as possible, and chose to use my religion as her weapon. Needless to say, I walked out. It's impossible to have an honest conversation with someone who isn't interested in engaging in one.

During a televised CNN Presidential Town Hall, CNN host Dana Bash seemed to be doing her best to foment anti-Hindu religious bigotry in a "question" she asked me, sounding a dog whistle to alert voters that there is something suspect about my religious beliefs and therefore I am not to be trusted.

The hypocrisy of the Democrat elite and their friends in the propaganda media is stark. On the one hand, they scream and shout about religious bigotry when it's politically or monetarily beneficial to them. On the other hand, they don't think twice about fomenting religious bigotry when doing so serves their interests.

Grace Will Lead Me Home

On the morning of June 18, 2015, we woke up to devastating news about a ghastly mass shooting at a historic church in Charleston, South Carolina, that had occurred the night before. A lone gunman had walked into the basement of Mother Emanuel AME Church in Charleston, a historic African Methodist Episcopal church dating back to the early 1800s, and murdered nine people.

The shooter was a twenty-one-year-old self-proclaimed neo-Nazi white supremacist named Dylann Roof. He had chosen Mother Emanuel AME Church as his target because it was a site historically meaningful to the African American community; a place where enslaved and free blacks had gone to worship together and worked to build a plan to free all who were still enslaved. In a city filled with historic monuments, Roof chose this church as the site for what he hoped would be the shot that would spark a race war across the country.

On the evening of June 17, 2015, Roof walked into the basement of the historic Mother Emanuel AME Church and was welcomed by those who were gathering for their regularly scheduled Bible study. Then Roof pulled out his pistol and started shooting. At one point, a young man named Tywanza Sanders stood up, trying to protect those around him, and confronted Roof, asking him why he was doing this. Roof responded, "I have to do this because ya'll are raping our women and taking over the world." Then he aimed his gun at Tywanza and pulled the trigger five times, watching as he took his last breath.

Dylann Roof killed nine people that day, injured a tenth person, and then fled.

The following morning, Roof was apprehended by police roughly 245 miles north of Charleston. In his car was a list of several more churches that he intended to be his next targets.

What happened next was nothing short of a miracle that could only be possible through the grace and power of God's love.

Two days after the shooting, Dylann Roof was arraigned at his first court appearance, and many family members of those killed by Roof were present. I expected to see tear-filled heartbreak and anger expressed toward this total stranger who had abruptly walked into a church and taken the lives of those they love.

But that's not what happened.

Ethel Lance was one of the victims—seventy years old, she left behind five children, seven grandchildren, and four great-grandchildren. One of her daughters courageously stood up and spoke directly to Roof in the courtroom, saying, "I will never be able to hold her again. But I forgive you and have mercy on your soul. It hurts me, and it hurts a lot of people, but God forgives you, and I forgive you."

Tywanza Sanders's mother was at the Bible study and saw her son shot and killed point-blank. She stood up and said, "We welcomed you Wednesday night in our Bible Study with open arms. You have killed the most beautifulest people I know. Tywanza Sanders was my son, but Tywanza was my hero. But as we said in Bible Study, we enjoyed you, but may God have mercy on your soul."[16]

This powerful and beautiful expression of love and forgiveness broke through the overwhelming prison of grief and brought light, not only to that courtroom, but to a nation in darkness.

Just two days after this unspeakable tragedy, at a time when many people who had endured such tragic loss would have a hard time just getting out of bed and leaving the house, these people found the strength to go to that courtroom and open their hearts to forgive the man who just forty-eight hours earlier was so filled with hate that he walked into a Bible study and took the lives of nine strangers.

They were living examples of what the Reverend Martin Luther King Jr. preached: "Returning hate for hate multiplies hate, adding deeper darkness to a night already devoid of stars. Darkness cannot drive out darkness; only light can do that. Hate cannot drive out hate; only love can do that."[17]

I was overwhelmed with emotion as I watched this incredibly powerful expression of love. Through the tears in their eyes, and the seemingly endless pain of such devastating loss, I felt an outpouring of love flowing from their hearts. There was only one place, one person that could give them the strength to forgive the unforgivable: our most merciful, most kind, loving God. Only through the immeasurable power of God's mercy, grace, and love could anyone find the path to forgiving a person who had committed this most heinous, hate-filled crime.

Nine days after the shooting, I joined my friend Congressman Trey Gowdy in South Carolina for the memorial service. As we drove down the cobblestone streets of Charleston on the way to the TD Arena where the service would be held, Trey pointed out different sites that stood out as daily reminders of the history of slave trading that had occurred on those very streets. He told me about the Old Slave Mart at 6 Chalmers Street where men, women, and children were dragged in chains, stood up on three-foot-high tables, and auctioned off to the highest bidder as though they were nothing but pieces of equipment.

As we entered the arena, we stopped in one of the team locker rooms where Trey, Senator Tim Scott, and I visited for just a few moments, holding hands in quiet prayer. I could hear the beautiful voices of the Mother Emanuel AME Church choir floating through the halls. In that dim locker room, we shared our own heartfelt expressions of gratitude to God, for His unconditional love and mercy, and for bringing so many souls together from across the country on this day to celebrate Him and the lives of those who had been murdered just a few days before.

As a nation, we grieved. In God's love, we found peace.

As we entered the stadium and found our seats, there were already thousands of people there, lifting their voices in praise and worship, responding to the calls of the choir. Their voices echoed off every wall with a spiritual force that could only be felt in a gathering of hearts united in their praise of God. I was reminded of lyrics from "The Wedding Song" that my dad sang to my mom when he married her: "The union of your spirits here has caused Him to remain / For whenever two or more of you are gathered in His name / There is love."[18]

The warm embrace of God's unconditional love surrounded us all. Nothing else mattered. The race, gender, and politics of everyone gathered that day didn't matter. We stood as one— family, friends, fellow Americans, children of God, opening our hearts to the grace of God's love.

The service closed with thousands of voices joining together in a powerful rendition of "Amazing Grace."

Amazing grace how sweet the sound
That saved a wretch like me,
I once was lost, but now I'm found
Was blind but now I see.

'Twas grace that taught my heart to fear
And grace my fears relieved.
How precious did that grace appear
The hour I first believed.

Through many dangers, toils, and snares
I have already come.
'Tis grace that brought me safe thus far
And grace will lead me home.

When we've been here ten thousand years
Bright, shining as the sun
We've no less days to sing God's praise
Than when we first begun.

I don't remember who was standing to my left and right, but we held hands, and I closed my eyes as I sang, tears streaming down my face.

On Memorial Day and every day, I honor my brothers and sisters who have paid the ultimate price.

During each of my three deployments to war zones, and in my travels today, my guitalele is never far away!

IS TODAY
THE DAY

NO U.S. PERSONNEL BEYOND
THIS POINT WITHOUT
WEAPON ·IBA· KEVLAR
O PT UNIFORM ALLOWED

Seeing this sign almost every day while I was deployed in Iraq in 2005 constantly reminded me that any day could be my last.

I didn't fully understand the stress my parents felt during my deployment until I came home. I had never seen my dad cry until the day I ran into his arms after serving in Iraq for a year. He held me tighter than ever and cried tears of relief and joy.

Immersed in the glory
of the morning sun

Resting in the warmth
of God's unconditional love

Renews our strength
Inspires our hearts

To share that love
To live that love
To act on that love
To serve.

As the fourth of five kids, I'm grateful for the real-world education I had growing up, including being homeschooled by my parents and working in our family's deli. My job was to wipe the tables, sweep the floor, and greet customers as they came in the door!

We stand on the shoulders of giants who sacrificed so much in defense of our nation and our freedom. I'm honored to have spent time with survivors of the attack on Pearl Harbor, joining them to commemorate those killed on that fateful day.

Caring for our *ʻāina* (land), *wai* (water), and community is what inspired me to get involved with politics when I was twenty-one years old.

Ever since I was a kid, the ocean has always been a place of peace, respite, and fun. It became even more special when my husband, Abraham, proposed to me at one of our favorite surf spots!

In the midst of the darkness of this tragedy, the amazing power of God's love shined brightly, showing us all—Democrats or Republicans, black, brown, or white, Christian or Hindu, male or female—the way to unite our country. We're all God's children. Appreciation of this fact is the glue that holds our country together as one nation under God. Remove this invisible transcendental power of spiritual love, and the dark forces of hate, greed, and corruption will tear apart the fabric of our country. Unfortunately, it's already begun.

The Bottom Line

We are facing a spiritual crisis in America, and it is tearing us apart. Our country's founding principles were written into the heart of the Declaration of Independence.

> **We hold these truths to be self-evident, that all men are created equal, that they are endowed by their Creator with certain unalienable Rights, that among these are Life, Liberty and the pursuit of Happiness.**

This is the spiritual foundation of our Constitution and the moral construct of our country. When that spiritual foundation is destroyed, the demise of our country will be here.

The First Amendment requires the government to respect and protect our God-given right to choose to have a personal relationship with God, and to express that faith however we choose without fear of state-sponsored reprisal, censorship, or discrimination—as well as the right to choose to have no faith, religion, or spiritual practice at all.

Unfortunately, today's Democrat Party does not believe in freedom. **They reject the Constitution, which recognizes that our rights come from God—not from the government.**

To acknowledge that our rights are granted to us by a power that transcends man, government, and any other institution, is to acknowledge that no man, government, or institution has the authority to take away our rights. When we, the people, appreciate that our rights are granted to us by a higher power, then we will naturally revolt when any man, government, or institution tries to take our rights away, knowing full well they have no authority to do so.

To overcome this obstacle, those who want to amass greater power and control over the people see that their first task must be to undermine our love, faith, and trust in God and somehow convince us, with either a carrot or a stick, that we must place our faith and trust in them instead of God or a higher power. After all, the very concept of our rights being "unalienable" (which by definition means "unable to be taken away from") because they are bestowed upon us by a transcendent power is predicated upon the existence of such a transcendent power. If you get rid of that foundation, everything resting upon that foundation crumbles.

This is the reason why the Democrat elite are so hell-bent on removing God from every facet of our lives. Their goal is to amass greater power and control over us. Therefore, their first task must be to undermine our love, faith, and trust in God, and somehow convince us, with carrot and stick, that we must instead place our faith and trust in them instead.

Nothing is more dangerous to our freedom than leaders of a political party who want to be more powerful than God.

They are envious of God and see Him as their primary competitor in their desire to become the Supreme Controller themselves. In this sick state of mind, they find joy in being the master who lords over others, gaining pleasure from forcing people to do their will. They want us to see them as God, worshipping, loving, and obeying them.

This is why they have a vested interest in trying to erase any mention of God in our public life. They need to try to sideline God because they want to be God. They want us to listen to them, and them alone. In their quest for control and power, they cannot have people guided by their own consciences, which comes from God.

Whether they admit it or not, they are threatened by God because God is love, and there is nothing more powerful than love. Those who choose to have a relationship with God draw happiness, inner strength, and confidence from His love. But the Democrat elite don't want us to be strong, confident, happy, and fearless. Why? Because it's a lot easier to control people who are weak and afraid. They are afraid of those who find the inner spiritual strength that comes from God because we have the courage and willingness to take a stand for what is right, speak the truth, and reject those who are trying to control us in their own pursuit of power.

Those who have a relationship with God and recognize that real happiness is found in loving God are not tempted by the shiny trinkets dangled before us, nor bullied by the sticks they beat us with. No matter what tactic they use to try to force us to reject God and what He is telling us in our hearts, they will fail. Our relationship with God and our desire to please to Him is far greater than the worldly rewards and punishments they have the power to levy.

To be antagonistic toward God, spirituality, and people of faith is to be antagonistic toward the foundation of the freedoms enshrined in our Constitution. Anyone, and any party, that embodies such hostility cannot be trusted to protect our inalienable God-given rights enshrined in the Constitution and should not be in power.

I could not in good conscience be associated with such a party, so I am no longer a Democrat.

CHAPTER FIVE

The Elitist Cabal of Warmongers

I can no longer remain in today's Democrat Party, which is now under the complete control of an elitist cabal of woke warmongers who have led us to the brink of nuclear war.

The world is closer to a nuclear holocaust than at any time in our history.

How did we get here?

It is the result of the insatiable self-serving desire of Hillary Clinton and the Democrat Party Elite for power. It is a result of their willingness to sacrifice the national security, safety, and well-being of the American people, and the world, in order to win the 2016 presidential election. Their strategy was simple: use their propaganda media and the national security state to stoke and heighten a New Cold War with

Russia, portraying Putin as the new Hitler, and then destroy Trump by tying him to Putin.

> Hillary Clinton: Donald Trump would be Putin's "puppet."
> —CNN[1]

> From the moment he waded into the 2016 presidential race, Donald Trump has behaved like a pro-Russia agent.
> —MSNBC[2]

> "I think it's possible" that Trump is a Russian asset
> —Andrew McCabe, former acting FBI director[3]

> Donald Trump Was Everything Vladimir Putin Could Have Wished For.
> —*New Republic*[4]

I can no longer be associated with the Democrat elite so willing to jeopardize our freedom, our prosperity, and the very existence of the American people, our country, and the world by pouring gasoline on the fire of the New Cold War in order to satisfy their self-serving ambitions. Their actions sicken me.

This Is Not a Drill

On the morning of January 13, 2018, the sun rose in Hawaii around seven o'clock, bringing a soft orange glow to the empty streets. Surfers on dawn patrol paddled out into the glistening water, sitting up on their boards, waiting in silence for the waves to come. On the beach, hotel workers lined up white chairs in the sand for the tourists just beginning to emerge from their hotels. For a few minutes, it seemed like just another lazy Hawaii weekend was beginning.

But it wasn't. This would turn out to be a day we would never forget.

I had been a member of Congress for just over five years, representing Hawaii's second congressional district, which included every island in the state of Hawaii except for the urban corridor of Honolulu. I often returned to Hawaii from Washington for district work on the weekend, but this was one of those rare weekends when I was in Washington, D.C., sitting at home on the couch with my laptop and steaming hot bowl of miso broth and ramen, looking forward to a quiet afternoon of reading and work.

My phone buzzed. I saw a text from Emily, my press secretary, who was working in our district office that week.

"Just got this," it read.

Nothing else came through. I had an uneasy feeling that something was terribly wrong. I called right away.

She didn't answer.

I pulled up Twitter and checked for breaking news. Nothing. I scanned the headlines of the *New York Times*, *Washington Post*, and other papers; nothing stood out.

I tried calling Emily again. This time she answered, though she could barely speak.

"Did you see it?"

Emily sounded panicked.

I put the phone on speaker, returned to our text thread, and then saw a screenshot she had taken come through.

I caught my breath.

"BALLISTIC MISSILE THREAT INBOUND TO HAWAII. SEEK IMMEDIATE SHELTER. THIS IS NOT A DRILL."

I was stunned. This was it. Throughout my time in Congress, as a member of the House Armed Services Committee, I had been sounding the alarm bells about North Korea's increasing missile and nuclear capabilities, calling for more effective missile defense systems and for negotiations to deescalate tensions and ultimately denuclearize the Korean peninsula—a goal that still appeared within reach at the time. As I looked at that image on my phone, I stopped breathing, envisioning a thousand different disasters: nuclear mushroom clouds, buildings collapsing, flashes of hot white light obliterating my family. I thought of my parents, who were probably just getting up and settling in for their morning solitude time in prayer. I thought of my friends and family, five thousand miles away.

The alert said, "SEEK IMMEDIATE SHELTER."

But there was a major problem: There were no shelters for anyone to escape to. There was no place for Mom and Dad to run to and be safe. There was no shelter for anyone in our state—except possibly the governor and highest-level officials. There were no underground bunkers—certainly none that would protect anyone from the blast of a nuclear attack, the nuclear fallout, or the nuclear winter that would follow.

"SEEK IMMEDIATE SHELTER. THIS IS NOT A DRILL."

I was overwhelmed with so many feelings, but most of all utter helplessness and dread. The unimaginable was happening. Those I love most in this world would have just minutes to live before being annihilated by an incoming missile from North Korea, and I wasn't there with them. Would I even be able to reach my parents to tell them that I loved them one last time?

Emily was still on the phone, and couldn't move. She was terrified, cowering in the bathtub, voice shaking: "I don't know what I'm supposed to do."

Few of my colleagues in Congress took my warnings about the increasing threat from North Korea seriously. Democrats were too

busy accusing President Trump of being a Russian agent or collabo-
rator. Many Republicans and pundits on TV glibly brushed off the
North Korea threat as something unimportant, not worth their time.
Even as reports of North Korea's increasing capabilities, missile and
nuclear, continued to come across our desks in Congress, nothing got
their attention. It blew my mind. How could they not recognize the
seriousness of this threat to the United States? Still, I persisted, eventually succeeding in urging my colleagues to install a Homeland Defense
Radar system for the protection of Hawaii.

But on this day, as the alarm sounded, there was no defense.

Panic and terror overwhelmed people all across Hawaii as tourists
and residents alike heard or saw the message:

**"BALLISTIC MISSILE THREAT INBOUND TO HAWAII. SEEK
IMMEDIATE SHELTER. THIS IS NOT A DRILL."**

Now, I want you, the reader, to stop for just a moment and think.
Wherever you are right now . . . sitting on the couch at home reading
this book, or maybe listening to it as you're driving to work or doing the
dishes at home. Imagine you hear an alert on your cell phone and when
you check it you see this message. How would you feel? What would run
through your mind at this very moment? Where are your kids, husband or
wife, parents? How much time do you have? Can you get to them in time?
Where will you go, right now, knowing you have possibly fifteen or twenty
minutes until the missile hits? The basement? The bathtub? The local community center? None of these places will protect you or your loved ones.

On that Saturday morning in Hawaii, everyone was confronted
with this terrifying reality.

CCTV footage captured images of college students at the University
of Hawaii sprinting across campus, running in fear, trying in vain to
open locked doors to the library, the campus center, and any other
structure made of concrete, trying desperately to find shelter. There
was none.

Families gathered their children and huddled in bathtubs or hunkered down in dark closets. My friend Jason left me a message saying that he was packing up his wife and seven children in the minivan and driving to Waianae on the west side of Oahu to hide in a cave. I later heard from a father who sat crying in his car because as the alarm sounded, he was near the middle of the island with one of his children twenty minutes away on the west side of the island and the other twenty minutes away on the east side of the island. He was frozen in place facing the most impossible dilemma—how could he choose which of his children he would drive to and spend the last minutes of his life with?

A video was posted on Twitter of a father in Honolulu who lowered his seven-year-old daughter into an open manhole, telling her to stay down there no matter what, and saying, "I hope I see you again."

I hung up with Emily and immediately called the state adjutant general, Major General Joe Logan, who was also the civil defense director for the state. He answered right away. I asked him, "What's going on?" He was curt in his response: "It's a false alarm. Someone pushed the wrong button." I said, "Just to confirm, there is no missile inbound?" He said, "Correct, there is no missile inbound."

People needed to know this information immediately. I grabbed my phone and quickly typed out a tweet, including the image of the alert, saying:

HAWAII—THIS IS A FALSE ALARM. THERE IS NO INCOMING MISSILE TO HAWAII. I HAVE CONFIRMED WITH OFFICIALS THERE IS NO INCOMING MISSILE.[5]

Then I called my dad. He answered immediately with a frantic, "Hello?!" He had me on speaker with Mom hovering next to him. I said, "There is no attack. Someone pushed the wrong button. There is no attack. I love you guys. I have to go and let other people know." I hung up and started dialing again.

My tweet was the first notification to the people of Hawaii that
there was no attack.

While officials knew this information sooner, the governor failed
to let people know immediately that
there was no attack because he had
forgotten his Twitter password.

As word spread, everyone breathed
a sigh of relief that this was a false
alarm. But the fact remained: we
reacted the way we did because the
threat of nuclear war was and is
real and is even greater today. This
should have been a wake-up call not
only for the people of Hawaii but for
our country. Unfortunately, very few
actually did wake up.

We face the harsh reality, with escalating cold wars being waged
with Russia and China, two nuclear-armed nations, that just a spark
could kick off a nuclear war, intentionally or unintentionally because
of a miscalculation. Our leaders know this fact. The Doomsday Clock
that's adjusted every year by the Bulletin of the Atomic Scientists is
currently set to ninety seconds before midnight—the closest to global
catastrophe it has ever been.[6]

Civil Defense systems in towns and cities across the country have
pre-drafted alerts similar to the one in Hawaii ready to go out at the
press of a button in the event of such an attack that tell us to "SEEK
IMMEDIATE SHELTER." But they don't tell people where shelter
can be found.

Trust me, the world's political and financial elite have access to bunkers to protect themselves and their loved ones from a nuclear blast and ensuing fallout. Politicians have plans in place to protect themselves so they can continue to wage a nuclear war from underground in the event of such an attack.

But what about the rest of us? We have nowhere to go. Our leaders failed us, driving us into this existential crisis, yet they have done nothing to protect us. They have not invested the hundreds of trillions of dollars that would be necessary to provide the American people with facilities that would offer even minimal protection from a nuclear attack and its aftermath. They don't care about us. We are left to be incinerated by the unimaginable white-hot blast of an exploding atom bomb. If by some miracle we survive that and the ensuing nuclear fallout, we will be left to endure the pain and suffering caused by radiation, no food and water, and a nuclear winter—leaving a barren landscape of death and destruction in the bomb's wake.

You would think that the horrific reality of this existential threat would naturally inspire our leaders to take urgent action to deescalate tensions with other nuclear-armed powers and walk us back from the brink of nuclear war. That's what anyone with any care or compassion in their hearts for the people would do.

But the warmongers in Washington from both political parties, their friends in the propaganda media, and bosses in the military-industrial complex nonchalantly brush off the threat of nuclear war as though it's nothing to be concerned about. It's insane! They go on television and talk about nuclear war as though it's just another battle where we can use this bomb or that missile, win the war, and move on. They lie to us about the consequences of their warmongering and where it could lead. They lie to us about the underlying reality: they are prepared to protect themselves but will leave the rest of us to be incinerated, should an attack occur.

One example of their lies and insanity was evident in a public service announcement the New York City Emergency Management Department released in July 2022.

Narrated by an attractive female actor in a cheerful voice, it begins with: "So there's been a nuclear attack. Don't ask me how or why; just know that The Big One has hit. So, what do we do?" With a smile on her face, she says, "There are three important steps that I want you to remember."

The three steps? "Get inside, stay inside, and stay tuned." She goes into detail on each one of the steps, continuing to smile as though the event of a nuclear attack is as normal as a bad winter storm. She encourages New York City residents to follow the Emergency Management Department on social media to get updates. Really??? After a nuclear blast that has completely destroyed the city, she's going to post a selfie video on Instagram saying, "Everything's fine! You can come out now!"?

To top it all off, she ends the video with a smile, saying with chirpy confidence: "All right? You've got this!"

Honestly, I didn't know whether to laugh or cry when I saw this. How is it possible these people are so far removed from reality that anyone would think this message was a good idea or that it made sense in any way at all? Sadly, it reflects the insanity of our leaders, intentionally misleading us and giving us a false sense of security that a nuclear attack is somehow survivable.

In 1985, when he was working with then Soviet president Mikhail Gorbachev to reduce the risk of nuclear war, Ronald Reagan made a statement that is just as true and relevant today as it was then: "A nuclear war can never be won and must never be fought."[7]

But the Democrat ruling elite apparently think otherwise. Either they are so ignorant that they think a nuclear war can actually be won, or they are so heartless and selfish that they intentionally deceive us as they forge ahead down a path of escalating New Cold Wars and a nuclear arms race that, if continued, can only lead to the complete destruction of humanity, all life, and the world as we know it.

How is it possible that our leaders have learned nothing from the past? How have they not learned from the many times during the height of the Cold War against the Soviet Union when a nuclear attack was almost launched because of mere misunderstanding? How have they not learned from the Cuban Missile Crisis, which was, in the words of one scholar, "the closest the world has ever come to complete annihilation"?[8]

In October of 1962, Nikita Khrushchev, the premier of the Soviet Union, ordered several nuclear missiles to be shipped into Cuba, which sits just over ninety miles from the shores of Florida. Knowing that this move put the safety of U.S. citizens and the sovereignty of the United States in jeopardy, President Kennedy knew he had to find a way to deescalate the situation and neutralize this threat. If just one of those missiles was launched—or if either side even *threatened* to launch a missile—the other side would respond in kind, beginning an irreversible chain of events that could lead to the extermination of humanity.

Ultimately, the crisis was averted because of President Kennedy's courageous leadership. He and Khrushchev recognized the mutually devastating consequences of a nuclear war, and after engaging in direct negotiations in secret, they agreed to a deal where Khrushchev would dismantle and remove the Soviet's nuclear weapons from Cuba so long as the United States agreed to two things: to remove its nuclear weapons from Turkey, which at that time shared a border with the USSR, and to commit to not invading Cuba. Thus, the world was pulled back from the brink of annihilation.

We can imagine, however, how easily things might have gone differently—if Bobby Kennedy, for instance, hadn't said exactly the right things during a last-minute meeting with the Soviet ambassador, or if President Kennedy had listened to and agreed with General Curtis LeMay, who insisted that military action was the only way out of the crisis.

Today's warmongers would have us believe that Kennedy was successful because he was the tough guy who went toe-to-toe, staring down Khrushchev until Khrushchev finally blinked and buckled to Kennedy's demands. But the truth is that Kennedy was quietly conversing and negotiating with Khrushchev behind the scenes, as they both understood the importance of peace and avoiding nuclear war. Their success was rooted in real diplomacy, which requires give and take.

Without diplomacy, there can be no peace. Without peace, we cannot be truly free or prosperous.

Ensuring that our military is strong, capable, and ready is essential to defending the security and freedom of our country. As a soldier for twenty years, and a Member of the House Armed Services Committee for nearly eight years, I know firsthand how critical this is.

The Great Seal of the United States, designed in 1782, reminds us of the importance of peace through strength. In its left talon, the bald eagle holds a bundle of thirteen arrows, symbolizing our military strength, and in the right talon an olive branch symbolizes our nation's commitment to seeking peace by exhausting all diplomatic efforts before using military force. The State Department describes this commitment, saying "The eagle always casts its gaze toward the olive branch signifying that our nation desires to pursue peace but stands ready to defend itself."[9]

Unfortunately, the warmongering Democrat elite and neocons deride those who seek peace as traitors or agents of the enemy, when in fact it is they who have rejected the values of our Founding Fathers and true patriots.

President John F. Kennedy's actions during the Cuban Missile Crisis are an example of the necessary balance between strength and a sincere willingness to use diplomacy, even if it means compromising in order to achieve peace and protect the safety, security, and freedom of the American people.

In a landmark address delivered shortly after the Cuban Missile crisis, President Kennedy spoke to graduates at American University about the need for U.S. foreign policy to make peace a priority.

"Above all," he said, "while defending our own vital interests, nuclear powers must avert those confrontations which bring an adversary to a choice of either a humiliating retreat or a nuclear war. To adopt that kind of course in the nuclear age would be evidence only of the bankruptcy of our policy—or of a collective death-wish for the world."[10]

I have read and reread this speech many times and get chills every time, listening to the audio, hearing the sincerity in President Kennedy's voice as he spoke not only to the graduating students, but to the American people and the world. His call to action then, decades ago, is a powerful call to action to every one of us today, as we sit, yet again, on the brink of nuclear war.

Unfortunately, as much as today's Democrat leaders pay lip service, praising President Kennedy as an iconic leader, the reality is they are not at all committed to achieving peace. They have instead chosen a path of war to serve their own personal, political, or financial interests. Being in a constant state of war creates an opportunity, which they readily exploit, to tighten the noose of government control over the people. With more control comes more power. And power is the only thing they care about.

The Big Lie

From the moment Democrats, some Republicans, and their propagandists in the mainstream media heard the fake story concocted and spread by Hillary Clinton about Trump "colluding" with Russia to "steal the election," they fell in line, no questions asked.

This was the beginning of what in effect has been a years-long coup d'etat against Trump, beginning during his 2016 campaign, continuing throughout his presidency, and is still being carried out today to try to stop him from being elected as president for a second time.

They recognized that as Trump's popularity grew in 2016, they needed a villain to attach him to, and for them, Vladimir Putin was the perfect enemy. With Russia as the enemy, they'd be able to gin up leftover feelings of fear and suspicion that remained from the last Cold War and easily use them to manipulate voters and raise suspicions about Trump.

Representative Adam Schiff, then the lead Democrat on the House Intelligence Committee, declared on national television that he had seen "more than circumstantial evidence" that Trump and his associates were colluding with the Russians to interfere in the U.S. elections. Other Democrats in Congress doubled down on this, repeating his statement. The truth is, there was no evidence, and Rep. Schiff knew that. They intentionally misled the American people hoping they would believe the false narrative that Trump was some kind of Manchurian Candidate for Putin—a puppet of a foreign dictator. They wanted the American people to believe that Trump couldn't be trusted; that he was not loyal to the American people.

Throughout this period, there were no Democrats in Congress who stood up for democracy and against this insanity. Every single Democrat from AOC to Bernie Sanders and the other so-called progressives toed the line, got on the anti-Russia, anti-Putin bandwagon, and essentially declared war. They knew they were undermining our democracy and our own safety and security by escalating tensions and sparking a New Cold War, but they forged ahead anyway. Most leading Democrats shared the dangerous sentiments expressed by Lieutenant General (retired) Mark Hertling in a *Politico* op-ed: "Putin's Attack on the U.S. is Our Pearl Harbor. Make no mistake: Hacking the 2016 election was an act of war. It's time we responded accordingly."[11] Respond accordingly? What does that mean, exactly? The United States responded to the attack on Pearl Harbor by declaring war against Japan on December 8, 1941. This costly, bloody war continued for years and only ended after the United States dropped two nuclear bombs on Japan in August of 1945.

The Japanese did not have nuclear weapons with which to respond and were forced to surrender. Russia, however, has approximately 5,977 nuclear weapons—more than any other country in the world, including the United States—that are many times more powerful than the atomic bombs used against Japan in World War II. They include strategic nuclear weapons capable of turning an entire country into ashes, and tactical nuclear weapons that are smaller, mobile, and still carry the same amount of power as the bombs dropped on Hiroshima and Nagasaki.

Voters saw through the lies about candidate Trump and elected him president in 2016 despite the Washington establishment's efforts to destroy him in order to get the queen of warmongers, Hillary Clinton, into the White House.

Even so, the powerful people who make up permanent Washington, including the national security state and propaganda media, were undeterred. They viewed Trump as a threat to their power and were determined as ever to continue working tirelessly to stop President Trump from executing his policies and responsibilities as president.

When you undermine the authority of the president, you take away the power the American people gave him to carry out his presidential duties. This, in effect, is a slow-rolling coup. The entire permanent Washington machine was activated to play their role in carrying this out: the Democratic National Committee, propaganda media, Big Tech, the FBI, the CIA, and a whole network of rogue intelligence and law enforcement agents working at the highest levels of our government. If you weren't already aware, when you hear people talking about the Deep State, this is who they're referring to. They collude and scheme to retain power, without regard for the wishes or interests of the American people.

The seriousness of what began in 2016 and continues now in the 2024 election as permanent Washington seeks to prevent voters from being able to choose who we want to vote for to be our next president cannot be overstated. Former president Trump remains the leading Republican candidate challenging President Biden's reelection bid. Fueled by their hunger for power and hatred for former president Trump, the Democrat elite are stealing our democracy and undermining the very foundation of our Republic before our very eyes.

Special Counsel John Durham spent more than two years investigating the Trump-Russia collusion narrative. His report, released on May 15, 2023, painstakingly covered the steps that the FBI took to prosecute Donald Trump even as it protected Hillary Clinton and members of her campaign. It was devastating to the FBI. After being exposed, even corrupt leaders of the FBI admitted their own wrongdoing. Jake Tapper, who'd suggested many times that it was only a matter of time before it was proven that Trump had ties to Russia, admitted that the report "does exonerate Donald Trump."

Shortly after the report was released, John Durham testified in front of Congress, where he spoke about the extent to which Hillary Clinton and her campaign created the Trump-Russia narrative and pushed it to the public, knowing all the while that it was false.

Asked by Representative Jim Jordan whether our government, in the summer of 2016, received intelligence "that suggested [Hillary] Clinton had approved a plan to tie President Trump to Russia," Durham said yes. He also noted that James Comey refused to share that information with the FBI agents who were working on Crossfire Hurricane, the investigation into Trump's ties to Russia.

The Durham report confirmed what many of us saw all along—that the Trump-Russia hoax was an escalation of the New Cold War that Democrats were and are waging to destroy Trump and get more power.

In 2018, President Trump said that "getting along with Russia is a good thing."[12] As you might imagine, the Democrats and permanent Washington went crazy. How dare he make such a traitorous statement?! It went against everything that they were working toward—a New Cold War against Russia. God forbid Trump have a relationship where conflict could be resolved peacefully. Democrats don't want a peaceful relationship with Russia at all. If Trump were successful, who would be the Democrats' boogeyman? How would their friends in the military-industrial complex make trillions of dollars from the fear they fomented in America and Europe by stoking the fires of the New Cold War?

Add this to yet another of the long list of reasons that Democrats and permanent Washington hate Trump so much. He wasn't willing to go along with their war plans. He exposed them for who they really are: they don't care about peace. They are driven by greed and a desire for more power, and they need war to achieve that. So, their game plan is to increase confrontation, conflict, push for regime change, and wage a New Cold War that has turned into a hot proxy war against Russia, despicably using the Ukrainian people as cannon fodder. The Biden administration refuses to support negotiations to end that war, because ultimately they don't care about the people of Ukraine. And they don't care about the safety, security, and freedom of the American people.

Trump stands in the way of their heinous plans, so they will stop at nothing to destroy him, and in doing so put our democracy, freedom, and our very existence on the line.

The War Uniparty

Washington is consumed with hyper-partisanship and divisiveness, but there is one issue that consistently brings many Republicans and Democrats together: war. Neocons and neolibs coming together to make up the Washington war uniparty.

In his presidential farewell address on January 17, 1961, President Eisenhower, a retired five-star Army general, warned the American people about the consequences of a cozy relationship between Congress, the executive branch, and the military-industrial complex: "In the councils of government, we must guard against the acquisition of unwarranted influence, whether sought or unsought, by the military-industrial complex. The potential for the disastrous rise of misplaced power exists and will persist."[13]

He was right. In the sixty years since President Eisenhower delivered this warning, the influence of the military-industrial complex and the national security state has grown to dangerous and costly levels. A recent study reported that defense contractors pocketed nearly half of the $14 trillion spent by the Department of Defense since 9/11.[14]

Without any regard for the cost in human lives or taxpayer dollars, Democrat and Republican leaders have stood together, waging one regime-change war after another for decades. Now, they want to see regime change in Russia and China.

They don't care that regime change in Russia would likely destabilize the whole country, impact global food and energy supplies, and most dangerously, leave thousands of nuclear weapons unsecured and vulnerable to being traded and used by who knows who against the United States or our allies.

They also don't care, or seem oblivious, that their regime-change war against China could have a catastrophic effect on American and world economies, undermine stability across the Asia-Pacific, and likely lead to a resurgence of competing provincial warlords in China rising to power, many possessing nuclear weapons, and thus posing an existential threat to the United States, neighboring countries, and the world.

After the nuclear wake-up call in Hawaii, I took every opportunity to continue sounding the alarm about the threat of nuclear war. On television, radio shows, and in speeches, I talked about how the increasing nuclear threat from North Korea was directly connected to our country's regime-change wars, and therefore, about the need to change our foreign policy.

I reminded people that Kim Jong-Un came to power the same year that former secretary of state Hillary Clinton led the overthrow of Muammar Gaddafi in Libya. North Korean leaders saw Gaddafi surrender his nuclear weapons program after the American invasion of Iraq in exchange for a promise that the United States would not topple his government. The reward for this act of "good behavior" was for the Obama administration, at the urging of Hillary Clinton, to lead a military attack against Gaddafi, topple him from power, and see him beaten, bloodied, dragged through the streets, and killed. Hillary Clinton responded to the news of his death with bloodcurdling laughter as she joked with a CBS reporter, declaring, "We came, we saw, he died!" Libya became a failed state, with slave trading in open markets, and Islamist terrorists took control of vast swaths of territory.

It doesn't take a foreign policy expert to recognize how our country's ongoing regime-change war policy directly undermines our national security and our efforts to prevent the proliferation of nuclear weapons. Kim Jong-Un did not want to end up like Gaddafi. He saw nuclear weapons as his regime's ultimate deterrence against U.S.-led regime change. Any promise made to North Korea that there would be no attempt to topple Kim's regime if he gave up nuclear weapons would be rejected outright. As North Korea had watched the overthrow of Gaddafi happen in real time, a North Korean foreign policy official made this anonymous statement: "The Libyan crisis is teaching the international community a grave lesson," and referred to Libya's disarmament deal with the United States as "an invasion tactic to disarm the country."

When I announced my candidacy for president on February 2, 2019, I made it clear that as commander in chief, my top priority would be to end our regime-change wars, the New Cold War, and the nuclear arms race, and that I would reduce the threat of nuclear war. I would engage directly with allies and adversaries alike to reduce tensions, negotiate treaties of collective security, and promote peace.

Almost every day of my campaign, I shared the story of the missile alert in Hawaii, and I posed to those attending my town hall meetings the same question I asked of you: "If you were to get that alert on your phone right now, 'MISSILE INCOMING, SEEK SHELTER IMMEDIATELY,' knowing you had just fifteen minutes to live, where would you go? Where would you find shelter?" The silence in every one of these town halls in cities and towns across the country was deafening. Every. Single. Time. Because they realized, as we did in Hawaii, that there is no shelter.

I spoke about the need for real leadership to do the hard work of diplomacy to bring about peace and stop the Washington establishment from escalating tensions with other nuclear-armed nations.

Before you assume that such a mission is naive, or that it fails to recognize the real threats and tough realities of the global community we live in, I ask you to reflect on President John F. Kennedy's words from his June 10, 1963, commencement address at American University:

> What kind of peace do I mean? What kind of peace do we seek? Not a Pax Americana enforced on the world by American weapons of war. Not the peace of the grave or the security of the slave. I am talking about genuine peace, the kind of peace that makes life on earth worth living, the kind that enables men and nations to grow and to hope and to build a better life for their children—not merely peace for Americans but peace for all men and women—not merely peace in our time but peace for all time.
>
> I speak of peace because of the new face of war. Total war makes no sense in an age when great powers can maintain large and relatively invulnerable nuclear forces and refuse to surrender without resort to those forces. It makes no sense in an age when a single nuclear weapon contains almost ten times the explosive force delivered by all the allied air forces in the Second World War. It makes no sense in an age when the deadly poisons produced by a nuclear exchange would be carried by wind and water and soil and seed to the far corners of the globe and to generations yet unborn.
>
> First: Let us examine our attitude toward peace itself. Too many of us think it is impossible. Too many think it unreal. But that is a dangerous, defeatist belief. It leads to the conclusion that war is inevitable—that mankind is doomed—that we are gripped by forces we cannot control.
>
> We need not accept that view. Our problems are manmade—therefore, they can be solved by man. And man can be as big as he wants. No problem of human destiny is beyond human beings. Man's reason and spirit have often

solved the seemingly unsolvable—and we believe they can do it again.

I am not referring to the absolute, infinite concept of peace and good will of which some fantasies and fanatics dream. I do not deny the value of hopes and dreams but we merely invite discouragement and incredulity by making that our only and immediate goal.

Let us focus instead on a more practical, more attainable peace—based not on a sudden revolution in human nature but on a gradual evolution in human institutions—on a series of concrete actions and effective agreements which are in the interest of all concerned. There is no single, simple key to this peace—no grand or magic formula to be adopted by one or two powers. Genuine peace must be the product of many nations, the sum of many acts. It must be dynamic, not static, changing to meet the challenge of each new generation. For peace is a process—a way of solving problems.

With such a peace, there will still be quarrels and conflicting interests, as there are within families and nations. World peace, like community peace, does not require that each man love his neighbor—it requires only that they live together in mutual tolerance, submitting their disputes to a just and peaceful settlement. And history teaches us that enmities between nations, as between individuals, do not last forever. However fixed our likes and dislikes may seem, the tide of time and events will often bring surprising changes in the relations between nations and neighbors.

So let us persevere. Peace need not be impracticable, and war need not be inevitable. By defining our goal more clearly, by making it seem more manageable and less remote, we can help all peoples to see it, to draw hope from it, and to move irresistibly toward it.[15]

During the 2020 Democratic presidential primary, no other candidate wanted to address the consequences of the burgeoning New Cold War against Russia. No other candidate would address how, as commander in chief, they would deal with this threat, deescalate global tensions, and work toward peace. No cable TV hosts or debate moderators were willing to focus on the horrors we would face in the event of a nuclear attack. They didn't want to talk about it at all. Reporters covering my campaign rolled their eyes at me for bringing this issue up, time and time again. I remember walking offstage after a town hall meeting in New Hampshire, and one of them asked me why I was so "obsessed" with this issue. "It's *all* you talk about," she said.

During one of the presidential debates, every candidate on the stage was asked to name in one sentence the greatest threat facing the American people. I was the only one who said, "The greatest threat that we face is the fact that we're in a greater risk of nuclear war today than ever before in history." It brings me no pleasure to state that the warnings I sounded during the 2020 presidential primary have proven prescient.

The New Cold War

About two years after I suspended my campaign for the presidency, President Joe Biden traveled to New York City to speak at a private fundraiser for the Democrat Party. Near the end of the evening, he delivered a stunning pronouncement.

"For the first time since the Cuban Missile Crisis," he said, "we have a direct threat to the use of nuclear weapons, if in fact things continue down the path [they've] been going."[16] This was an understatement.

By October 2022, when President Biden delivered this off-the-cuff assessment to a crowd of big-dollar Democratic donors—not in a direct address to the American people—the war in Ukraine had claimed more than 100,000 lives in about eight months. President Vladimir Putin, who had ordered the invasion of Ukraine, stressed repeatedly that he would defend his country "by any means necessary." This was an obvious reference to the 5,977 nuclear warheads at his disposal, and his willingness to use them.

How did we get to this point?

No matter how strongly they deny it, President Biden, his administration, and the war uniparty in Washington do not care for peace, the people of Ukraine, or democracy. They are wholly uninterested in seeking a peaceful resolution to the Russian-Ukrainian war. Instead, they remain committed to achieving regime change in Russia. From Hillary Clinton's baseless lies about Donald Trump colluding with the Russians to President Biden's spending hundreds of billions of dollars to wage a proxy war against Russia through Ukraine, the Democrat elite are insistent on making the world a more dangerous place by putting their own selfish interests ahead of the national interests of the American people and our peace, security, freedom and prosperity.

Given the gravity of Biden's statement about the very real threat of nuclear war, a natural follow-up question anyone would ask is, *Mr. President, if this is true, then what are you doing to stop this war and support negotiations for peace? What are you doing to prevent World War III? What are you doing to prevent the American people from being annihilated in a nuclear war?*

But no one at that event asked the question. No one in the media asked that question. Not then, not now. No Democrat in Congress dares to challenge the Biden administration.

In the early weeks, even months, of the war in Ukraine, diplomacy remained a viable option and a pressing need—to end this conflict quickly before too many lives were lost, and cities destroyed. In March 2022, officials in Turkey sponsored talks between the governments of Russia and Ukraine. Representatives from both countries met, dialogue commenced, and there seemed to be a glimmer of hope that this could be the beginning of a diplomatic resolution to the conflict.

Suddenly, the Biden administration brought negotiations to a halt. According to recent revelations from Naftali Bennett, the former prime minister of Israel, it was "Western powers" that demanded that the peace talks stop so they could "continue to smash Putin."[17]

That same month, after an emergency NATO summit meeting in Brussels, President Biden flew to Warsaw, Poland, where he declared in unscripted remarks that Vladimir Putin "cannot remain in power."[18]

On April 25, 2022, U.S. Secretary of Defense Lloyd Austin summed up the Biden administration's position when he declared that the United States wanted "to see Russia weakened to the degree that it can't do the kinds of things that it has done in invading Ukraine."[19]

In early 2022, Congress *voted* on a $40 billion aid package for Ukraine—with many more billion-dollar packages to follow[20]—with no conditions on how the money would be used. Fifty-seven Republicans in the House and eleven Republican senators voted against it. Not a single Democrat opposed it.[21] Not one. Not one expressed reservation. Not one thought we should pause for a moment before involving the United States in a proxy war against the country that holds the most nuclear weapons in the world. I couldn't believe it.

Several months later, on October 22, 2022, as the proxy war raged on, thirty members of the Congressional Progressive Caucus, led by its chair, Congresswoman Pramila Jayapal, released a letter urging President Biden to seek a diplomatic resolution to the continuing conflict in Ukraine. When I heard the news, I thought maybe there was some hope for voices for peace in the Democrat Party after all.

The letter said, "Given the destruction created by this war for Ukraine and the world, as well as the risk of catastrophic escalation, we also believe it is in the interests of Ukraine, the United States, and the world to avoid a prolonged conflict. For this reason, we urge you to pair the military and economic support the United States has provided to Ukraine with a proactive diplomatic push, redoubling efforts to seek a realistic framework for a ceasefire."

The signatories noted, "The risk of nuclear weapons being used has been estimated to be higher now than at any time since the height of the Cold War. Given the catastrophic possibilities of nuclear escalation and miscalculation, which only increase the longer this war continues, we agree with your goal of avoiding direct military conflict as an overriding national-security priority."

In this letter, they requested that President Biden "make vigorous diplomatic efforts in support of a negotiated settlement and ceasefire, engage in direct talks with Russia, explore prospects for a new European security arrangement acceptable to all parties that will allow for a sovereign and independent Ukraine, and, in coordination with our Ukrainian partners, seek a rapid end to the conflict and reiterate this goal as America's chief priority."[22] The letter closed with the signatures of thirty Democrats in Congress.

Wow, I thought—maybe some Democrats do have the courage to stand up for peace.

But that hope was quickly shattered.

The reaction of the permanent Washington elite was immediate, fierce, and one-sided—on the side of war, of course. *Politico* and other news outlets deemed the letter "highly controversial," and just twenty-four hours after the progressive caucus sent the letter, they retracted it and blamed staff for releasing it without their approval.[23] I was disgusted, to say the least. This is the usual excuse politicians use whenever they screw up and don't want to take responsibility—blame the staff.

The truth was, I knew what really happened, and it had nothing to do with "the staff." The Biden administration and the Democrat Party leadership cracked the whip, made some threats along the lines of, *Retract this letter, or face the consequences*, and these so-called progressives immediately buckled, did as they were told, and cowered in the corner. They showed their true colors. No matter how self-righteous their speeches on the House floor are, no matter how many times they denounce the military-industrial complex, when it comes right down to it, they care more about their own political ambitions and being in the good graces of the Democrat Party establishment than they do about peace, ending the suffering of the Ukrainian people, or preventing nuclear war.

It was clear that the Democrat Party was now truly under the complete control of an elitist cabal of warmongers and the military-industrial complex, and they demanded total compliance—or else.

Those of us who have the audacity to call for peace and an end to this war are immediately called Putin apologists or puppets. It's a way for the foreign policy establishment to try to discredit anyone who challenges them. The warmongers in Washington and their propagandists in the mainstream media are threatened by those of us who ask questions and tell the truth about the consequences of this war. They are afraid that the truth will expose their lies and the weakness of their position. So rather than engage in sincere dialogue or substantive debate, they immediately resort to smears and name-calling. They are afraid of the truth and afraid of a freethinking society. They will stop at nothing to silence and destroy us.

The collapse of the Soviet Union created an obvious opportunity to cultivate better relations with our former enemies, particularly Russia, with its immense nuclear arsenal. William J. Perry, secretary of defense under President Bill Clinton, recognized this and worked with Russian

Minister of Defense Pavel Grachev to reduce "much of the massive nuclear stockpile left over from the Cold War."

Recalling this collaboration, Perry wrote, "As the world's two largest nuclear powers, we viewed nuclear weapons stewardship as a joint responsibility. As part of this responsibility, we collectively dismantled approximately 9,000 nuclear weapons in both countries. Despite leftover bitterness from the Cold War, the U.S. government recognized that it was in the best interest of national security to provide financial support for the denuclearization effort."[24]

This effort continued, soon blossoming into an arrangement at NATO known as the "Partnership for Peace," which "allowed Russia and other European countries to work with NATO without becoming NATO members. This included joint peacekeeping operations that allowed Eastern European military units to work cooperatively with NATO military units."[25]

But this mission would be short-lived. President Clinton decided to expand NATO anyway, ignoring Russian objections and the warnings presented by his own secretary of defense, William Perry. When NATO expanded to include Poland, Hungary, and the Czech Republic, George Kennan—the dean of American diplomats who, at the beginning of the Cold War, had promoted a foreign policy of "containment" against the Soviet Union—warned that this action marked the beginning of a new Cold War.

Kennan, a conservative "realist," declared in the pages of *the New York Times* that expanding NATO would be "the most fateful error of American policy in the post-cold-war era."[26] He wrote: "Such a decision may be expected to inflame the nationalistic, anti-Western and militaristic tendencies in Russian opinion; to have an adverse effect on the development of Russian democracy; to restore the atmosphere of the cold war to East-West relations, and to impel Russian foreign policy in directions decidedly not to our liking. And, last but not least, it might make it much more difficult, if not impossible, to secure the Russian Duma's ratification of the Start II agreement and to achieve further reductions of nuclear weaponry."[27]

Kennan was proven correct.

Neither the Biden administration nor its allies in the media seem to appreciate that Russia remains a nuclear superpower. In the early months of the war between Ukraine and Russia, the *New York Times* published a disturbing exposé on the nuclear arsenal of Vladimir Putin. The tone of the article was bizarre. It treated the comparison of American and Russian nuclear stockpiles as something akin to comparing what shoes we had in our respective closets. The article utterly ignored the destructive power of even *one* of these missiles.

Given the seriousness of this nuclear threat, common sense would dictate a foreign policy that pursues peaceful coexistence with Russia. But permanent Washington's belligerent foreign policy needlessly pokes the Russian bear, escalating international tensions and, as a result, undermining the safety and security not only of the American people, but of the world.

The Cost of War

I deployed to Iraq in 2005 with the Hawaii National Guard's 29th Brigade Combat Team during the height of the war, serving in a field medical unit in a camp about forty miles north of Baghdad. Our security patrols faced almost daily ambushes and roadside bombs. A normal day in our camp included multiple mortar attacks launched toward us.

I led the Brigade Surgeon Operations Section where my first task, every day of the year that I was there, was to go through the list of Americans who had been wounded in combat in the previous twenty-four hours.

As I read each name on that list, my job was to identify any wounded soldiers assigned to our brigade of nearly three thousand people, find out where they were, and make sure they were getting the care they needed to stay in country and return to duty, or that they were being evacuated as quickly as possible to receive a higher level of care than we could provide in Iraq. Often their first destination would be either Ramstein or Landstuhl military hospital in Germany, followed by movement to Walter Reed Army Medical Center or some other military hospital in the United States.

My stomach was in knots every morning as I opened my laptop to check the list. Would there be anyone I knew on it? Whether I knew the names on that list personally or not, with every name, I knew there was a husband or wife at home worried sick, children missing their mom or dad, or parents sitting nervously by the phone praying that "the call" announcing the death or serious injury of their loved one would never come.

One day, I got word that one of our own had been killed.

Frank Tiai was from American Samoa and was a sergeant in the 100th Battalion, 442nd Infantry Regiment—a unit formed during World War II solely for Japanese American soldiers who wanted to prove their loyalty to America by enlisting to fight overseas, even though many had seen their loved ones being dragged out of their beds, classrooms, or jobs to be held in internment camps. The U.S. military often sent this unit ahead of the front lines to probe and clear enemy activity before the "real" U.S. Army came through. Their lives were viewed as expendable, and sadly, many were killed in combat. There were also many acts of stunning bravery. Twenty-one Japanese American soldiers in this unit earned the Medal of Honor. To this day, the 100th Battalion, 442nd Infantry Regiment is the most decorated infantry unit in the U.S. military.

On July 17, 2005, just one day before he was supposed to go home for two weeks of R&R leave, Sergeant Frank Tiai was out on a security patrol when he was hit by an improvised explosive device (IED) planted on the road, which detonated and killed him instantly.

When I got word of his death, I was overwhelmed with emotion. I slumped over and cried. I didn't know him very well, but the sense of loss I felt was real, and deep. I had seen Frank briefly the night before, walking out of the tent that was our makeshift gym. He had given me a nod and a quick smile as he went on his way. Now he was gone. Just like that.

We were at war. Death was a real possibility for any one of us on any given day. I knew that. We all did, to one degree or another. None of us knew when our day would come. I had made peace with that reality before I left home, writing final letters to my family, saying all the things I would want to say if I never saw them again.

Frank's death hit close to home. There were no final goodbyes. I thought of his family back in American Samoa. My heart broke for his wife and kids. They had been excited about his return, making plans for how they'd spend the short two weeks of vacation they'd have together. Now, suddenly, they had to plan his funeral.

Unfortunately, many more soldiers from our brigade would be killed in combat during that deployment. Many more American service members would sacrifice their lives in a war that was started by politicians who didn't care about them, or the loved ones they'd leave behind—an unnecessary and costly war that would undermine our nation's security, strengthen al-Qaeda, and lead to the birth of even more extreme Islamist terrorist groups like ISIS. As I grieved the loss of every one of my friends, wondering what this was all for, I thought of those politicians sitting in the safety of their fancy Washington offices, fat and happy, smoking their cigars, laughing their way to the bank with the money they got from their buddies in the military-industrial complex. They made me sick. And angry.

After Saddam Hussein was toppled and his government and military dismantled, the U.S. military took over Saddam's old Baghdad palaces and many of Iraq's military bases. Our camp was one of those, a former base for the Iraqi Army and Air Force. In the middle of it was an old movie theater. It wasn't in great condition; there were holes in an outdoor wall from mortar attacks, but it was the only hardened structure that would hold a few hundred people. As we filed in for Frank's memorial service, the air was thick with grief. The only sound was the shuffle of boots across the floor as we slowly found our seats. Two soldiers with ukuleles walked up the stairs and sat down on the stage. They started plucking the strings of their ukuleles and in low, soulful voices, they began to sing. Their haunting voices brought tears to my eyes, singing the melodic notes of a beautiful song called "Kamalani," which in Hawaiian means "heavenly child."

> He beckons you, Kamalani
> You'll be together again

As they finished singing, the First Sergeant stood and called his soldiers to attention with a booming voice. The final roll call began as he called the names of each of the soldiers in Frank's squad. As he called their names, each stood up and yelled, "Here, First Sergeant." And then, after a long pause, he called, "Staff Sergeant Tiai." No response.

He called out again, "Staff Sergeant Frank Tiai."

Silence.

One last time, he called out, "Staff Sergeant Frank Tiai."

Nothing.

The silence was deafening.

Frank was gone.

Then, in the corner of the theater, a door opened, the sunshine beaming through. The silence was shattered by the sharp crack of the three-rifle salute outside, firing again and again and again.

Our brother was gone.

At the front of the stage was a makeshift memorial—a simple fold-ing table set up with a framed picture of Frank, his eyes looking back at us with a slight smile on his face. Next to him were a pair of his empty boots, a rifle with the muzzle facing down, a helmet resting on top, and his military ID tags hanging on the side of the rifle. We lined up, each of us taking our turn to render our final salute to Frank, honoring his great sacrifice, and saying our final aloha and *a hui hou*—until we meet again, brother. The line was long, tears streaming down the cheeks of even our most hardened warriors.

Emerging from that theater, we went our separate ways. We went back to work. Duty called. We would grieve in our own ways, on our own time.

My eyes are wet with tears as I write these words, reliving the expe-rience as I share it with you. The memory of my brothers and sisters who never made the trip home never leaves me. They live on in our memories and in our hearts. The price they paid, the sacrifice they and their loved ones made, is impossible to measure. I do my best, every day that I am blessed to be alive, to honor their lives and their sacrifice.

It is in their memory that I fight with all that I have to stop corrupt, self-serving politicians from dishonoring the sacrifices of our military men and women by sending them to go fight in wars that have nothing to do with our nation's security—needlessly putting their lives at risk.

Every single one of us who raises our right hand and enlists in our Armed Services knows that in doing so we are volunteering to put our lives on the line to ensure the safety, security, and freedom of our country and the American people. That's a choice we make willingly. If and when that call comes, we stand ready to fulfill our commitment.

What we are not volunteering for is to serve as cannon fodder to fuel the profits of the military-industrial complex. We are not volunteer-ing to be used by insecure politicians who feel the need to start wars and put us in harm's way just to make themselves feel strong or look tough. We are not volunteering to be used as expendable pawns feeding the insatiable hunger for power and global domination of American politicians who don't care about our Constitution, our country, or the American people.

These very same politicians have the audacity to go and "visit the troops," using taxpayer-funded jets to fly to places like Iraq, Afghanistan, or now, Poland and Ukraine, staying for just long enough to shake a few hands, gripping and grinning, using our troops for a photo op they can put in their next campaign advertisement. And when they get back to Washington, they go on the news and talk soberly about how they've just "been to war." Give me a break. When they came to our camp in Iraq, I refused to shake their hands and be a part of their charade. They disgust me and anger me. They don't care about our troops. They don't care about our families. It's all lip service. Their actions tell the real story.

These politicians were responsible for the foreign policy disaster in Iraq that cost the United States trillions of dollars and the lives of nearly 4,500 Americans and another 32,000 wounded. According to a study published in 2008 by Opinion Research Business, it is estimated that more than one million Iraqi people died because of the war by that year.[28] Many more would die after. This number doesn't even include those who were killed and injured in Afghanistan. The politicians don't care. They feel it was "worth it."

Madeleine Albright was the U.S. ambassador to the United Nations appointed by President Bill Clinton, and later his secretary of state. She is someone the Democrat Party and mainstream media deify as a hero who can do no wrong.

When she was working as UN Ambassador, she successfully convinced the United Nations Security Council to place heavy sanctions on Iraq after the 1991 Gulf War, with the stated intent of punishing Saddam Hussein for invading Kuwait. The sanctions were maintained after Iraqi forces left Kuwait, to compel Hussein to pay war reparations and cooperate with United Nations weapons inspectors. But as always, those most hurt by the sanctions were not the powerful—Saddam Hussein and his cronies were largely unaffected. It was the innocent people of Iraq who paid the price.

During an interview with Madeleine Albright on *60 Minutes*, journalist Lesley Stahl cited a report on Iraqi civilian casualties attributable to the sanctions. "We have heard that half a million [Iraqi] children have died. I mean, that is more children than died in Hiroshima. And, you know, is the price worth it?" Madeleine Albright said yes. "I think that is a very hard choice, but the price, we think, the price is worth it."[29]

For too long, United States foreign policy has consisted of enacting crippling sanctions and waging regime-change wars, all under the banner of "defending freedom and democracy" around the world, and usually in the guise of humanitarianism. That was true under Democrat Bill Clinton, Republican George W. Bush, and Democrat Barack Obama. And true to form, President Biden has made waging a "global battle for democracy" against the rise of autocracies in the world the central pillar of his foreign policy agenda.[30]

The truth is, this worldview is based on the propagation of lies that set up a paradigm of good versus evil in the world, all so the war uniparty can have a mechanism—or an excuse—to feed their insatiable desire for more power and more money.

They tell the American people, and themselves, that their goal is so honorable and so great that the end justifies the means. If it means killing millions of people in order to "save" them, then that's what we have to do. As Madeline Albright put it, "It's worth it."

If we must destroy the United States—or the world—in order to save it, so be it.

The thing is, President Biden and his team reveal their hypocrisy as they decide which democracies they want to help and which autocracies they'll turn a blind eye to. They're more than willing to set aside their democracy crusade and cultural colonialism when it comes to countries like Turkey, Saudi Arabia, or Jordan. These countries are not democratic by any measure, and yet the U.S. government keeps them off their blacklist of autocratic enemies.

It's obvious these politicians don't actually care about democracies versus autocracies. What matters to them is who will submit to the will of the U.S. foreign policy establishment, and who refuses to bend the knee. That is where they draw the line. Those who refuse to bow are accused of rejecting the "rules-based order."[31] In plain English that means we create the rules, and the "good guys" are those who follow our rules, the "bad guys" are those who do not.

Why doesn't anyone ever ask the obvious question: what happens if other countries in the world apply this same "rules-based order" to their own foreign policy? What happens when they stand up and say, *No, respect our sovereignty. We don't want you to forcibly impose your American-style democracy, or radical LGBTQ+ woke agenda on us?* We know what happens. These countries are labeled "adversaries" or "the enemy" and they must be quashed and bullied into submission with economic or military warfare.

They apply the same strategy against "domestic enemies." Look at what they did to former president Trump in 2016 and 2020 and what they're doing to him now in the 2024 election. Just as they pick winners and losers when they orchestrate regime changes in other countries, they use the same tactics in our own elections, tilting the scales in favor of or against a certain candidate. They use their propaganda media, including social media, to portray their political opponents as an existential threat to our democracy, and then use the power of the national security state to destroy these so-called "domestic enemies."[32]

It's all part of the DNC playbook. They used it against me in 2020, and they're using it against Robert F. Kennedy Jr. in 2024. It's a three-step plan they deploy against candidates who refuse to fall in line.

First, they try to ignore you, as though you are not a candidate, and you don't exist. They do not want people to know you're running for president.

Second, if that doesn't work, they try to destroy your reputation, discredit you, and smear you, using their partners in the propaganda media. They try to define you before you have a chance to define yourself. They relentlessly publish one article after the next depicting you as a kook or fringe candidate so that voters will not take you seriously.

If that doesn't work, they go to step three—total destruction. They pull out all the stops to try to cancel to destroy you completely. It's what Hillary Clinton did to me when she started calling me a Russian asset, accusing me of being a traitor to the country that I love. They repeat baseless lies over and over until voters start to believe they're true.

We are seeing this play out once again with Donald Trump, but with him they are going much further. They are using the power of the gun—the power of law enforcement and the security state. They are so threatened by Trump that they are throwing everything and the kitchen sink at him to try to make it so that people will not even have the choice of voting for him. Biden's administration is using federal, state, and local law enforcement to go after his major political opponent in the middle of a presidential campaign, because they don't want voters to even have the option.

This is the kind of thing that happens in banana republics, where rulers are motivated by fear. It's not supposed to be happening in the United States of America, the land of the free, the home of the brave. But it is.

They claim to be the champions of democracy, yet they are undermining our democracy. They take away our liberties in the name of saving freedom. They censor information to "protect" us. They paint a target on the backs of anyone who dares to challenge their power, label them as "domestic terrorists,"[33] and destroy them.

Homecoming

Our flight home, after our yearlong deployment to Iraq, took us from Baghdad to Kuwait, a brief refueling layover in Ireland, and then to Texas, where we stayed at Fort Hood for a couple weeks to turn in equipment and receive endless PowerPoint redeployment briefings before boarding our final flight home to Hawaii. Our plane touched down at Hickam Air Force Base in the dark just before dawn. The excitement on that plane was palpable. We were finally home. As soon as they opened the doors and I took that first step down the stairs toward the tarmac, I stopped for a moment, closed my eyes, cherished the sweet Hawaii trade winds hitting my face, and listened to the chirping birds just starting to wake up.

We filed off the plane and started completing the final tasks that stood between us and our families. The crew assigned to the baggage detail got to work unloading one Army green duffel bag after another. We stood in a long line to turn in the rifles that had been our constant companions for the last eighteen months. Then, as the sun began to peek over the horizon, finally, we gathered in one mass formation, stood at the position of attention, and began our march into the hangar where our families were gathered, anxiously waiting. The excitement in the air was electric. We stood there, trying to maintain our military bearing, eyes forward, not moving a muscle, as our families were cheering and wildly waving "Welcome Home!" signs. Our commanding general delivered a short speech—I don't remember a single word he said, until he loudly called out, "Dismissed!" I had already figured out where my family was standing, and I immediately sprinted toward them, first, running straight into the warm embrace of my dad. I hugged him tighter than ever. As I did, I felt tears streaming down his face. My dad was crying. I had never seen my dad cry before. Then, I felt my mom join in, wrapping her arms around both of us, tears of joy flowing freely. At that moment, I fully realized how stressed and anxious they had been every day that I was away, a knot in their stomach every time they watched the evening news and heard reports of another soldier killed in Iraq. Finally, they could breathe a sigh of relief. I was home.

I was thrilled to be home. I had been gone for nearly eighteen months. I couldn't wait to get in the water. I couldn't wait to get back to my life—whatever that looked like. But the happiness I felt at being home was tempered by a conflicting deep sadness that weighed heavily on my heart. I shared how I felt with my family, and honestly, they were confused. How could one feel happiness and sadness at the same time? It didn't make sense. But the reality was, I couldn't feel completely happy knowing that there were seats on our plane left unfilled by our brothers and sisters who would never come home.

That deployment profoundly changed my life and how I viewed the world. I had experienced the harsh, unforgiving cost of war. I had witnessed the military-industrial complex at work, with the KBR Halliburton logo stamped on just about everything we touched in Iraq. From food to laundry to fuel to port-a-johns, the company made hundreds of billions, if not trillions more dollars in profit the longer the war raged on. I realized how we had been lied to and betrayed by our leaders, which came at an immeasurable cost: the loss of our friends, leaving behind a gaping hole in the hearts of their loved ones that could never be filled. The hardship of moms and dads sacrificing their sons and daughters in a faraway war. The cost of broken families that couldn't endure the hardship of the deployment—my first marriage ended as a statistic and casualty of this war.

Not Another War

When I returned home, many of my friends and former colleagues in the Hawaii statehouse assumed I would run for my old seat and resume the life I had left behind.

But I couldn't. Everything had changed. I had changed.

I felt compelled to find a way to use my experiences to influence our country's foreign policy and prevent self-serving politicians from continuing to wage senseless, costly, counterproductive regime-change wars. I wanted to be a force for peace and real security for my country.

Ultimately, this is what led me to campaign for a seat in the U.S. House of Representatives in 2012, where after a long and hard-fought campaign that most people believed was impossible for me to win, I became one of the first female combat veterans ever elected to Congress. I would go on to serve in Congress for eight years as a member of the Armed Services and Foreign Affairs Committees.

Seven months after I was sworn in as the representative for Hawaii's second congressional district, President Obama announced that he would seek congressional authorization to launch an attack that would be the first volley of a regime-change war in Syria. I was home in Hawaii at the time, as Congress was in recess. The day that this was announced, I was at a gas station filling up the tank when a woman approached me. Something was clearly wrong. As she began to speak, her voice was shaking and I could see the anxiety in her eyes. She put her hand on my arm and shared with me how her son had recently returned home from a tour of duty in Iraq. He was having a hard time finding his footing at home and struggled with post-traumatic stress. She was terrified that he might be sent to go fight in yet another war that didn't seem to make sense, and that she might lose him forever. With tears in her eyes, she squeezed my arm tightly and said, "Please, Tulsi. I know you have seen the ugliness of war. You know what my son is going through. Please, please, please, do not let them send my son

back over there. I'm afraid he won't make it home. I am begging you."
I'll never forget the look on her face—one of a mother protecting her
son, and terrified that he may be taken from her. It is a look that every
politician who wants to send our troops into harm's way should see.

Hearing her plea and having studied all the evidence the Obama
administration presented as they made their case to carry out an inter-
ventionist regime-change war in Syria, I publicly announced my opposition to such a war, pointing out that it would undermine our national
security, safety, and interests.

The next day, I got a call from Tina Tchen, First Lady Michelle
Obama's chief of staff. We had met once before but didn't know each
other well. I don't know why the administration chose her to be the one
to call me. Her voice was tense and angry. Her message was clear: *How
dare you? Who do you think you are? You are a freshman Democrat.
How dare you go against the president of your own party, and one
who is from your own home state, for gosh sakes?!*

At no time did she ask me about why I was opposed to President
Obama's intent to launch an attack in Syria. Neither she, nor President
Obama, nor anyone in the White House, was interested in having a
substantive conversation about my reasons for opposing the president's
plan to start a new war. They weren't interested in my experiences
serving in Iraq, the lessons I had learned, and how they informed my
views. It was an accusation of betrayal—not of my country or my fellow
servicemen and women, but of the Democrat Party and more personally, President Obama himself. Ms. Tchen's problem with me was that
I didn't support the president. I wasn't a team player.

The Bottom Line

Today's Democrat elite are willing to sacrifice the safety, security,
freedom, and economic well-being of the American people to advance

their own self-serving interests. They are willing to sacrifice peace and prosperity as a necessary cost of maintaining and increasing their power. They are willing to sacrifice the country I love, the American people, and the world on the altar of war. This is the main reason I could no longer be a Democrat.

Our nation is in desperate need of leaders who will make decisions based on what is in the best interests of the American people, guarding our nation's security, prosperity, and freedom. We need leaders who see the world as it is, not some fantasy world so many of our politicians seem to live in, where they think a nuclear war can be waged leaving us unscathed in the process.

We need leaders who will give up the age-old colonialist mindset that has been used to justify kinetic, economic, and cultural warfare around the world, often under the guise of lofty rhetoric about humanitarianism and spreading democracy, but which is really rooted in an arrogant view that we must remake the world in our image—whether people in other countries like it or not.

Our leaders must put the American people first. We must respect the sovereignty of other nations just as we expect them to respect our own. Our foreign policy should not be based on isolationism; instead, recognizing that the best way to achieve peace is by building relationships with other countries—not by dropping bombs or enacting crippling sanctions but rather through the common pursuit of mutual peace and prosperity that most world leaders seek for their own people, even if only for their own self-preservation. There will be differences and conflicts that must be dealt with, and we will be ready to defeat those who threaten our well-being, but war must always be the last resort.

How do we turn this imperative into reality?

As citizens, as voters, we hold the answer in our hands. Who we choose to lead our country has direct consequences on the question of war and peace.

With our voices, and our votes, we must hold corrupt, self-serving politicians accountable and let them know in no uncertain times that we will not allow them to destroy us, our loved ones, and our home.

As President Kennedy said, "Peace need not be impracticable, and war need not be inevitable." Don't let any warmongering politician convince you otherwise. Peace is not simply the absence of conflict, but something we must work at achieving every day.

We need leaders with foresight who will create an environment where diplomacy and dialogue replace emotional, knee-jerk reactions to global events—which so often lead to great harm and suffering and undermine our own economic and security interests.

We need leaders who are willing to engage with not only our friends, but more important, our adversaries. Diplomacy, when done correctly, is not a sign of weakness, as today's entrenched political class seems to believe; rather, it is the most effective tool for conflict resolution and the hallmark of a strong and confident nation.

To make this goal a reality, we must embrace the principle of service above self, in both our domestic and our foreign policy, and support those running for office who do their best to embody that spirit in all they do. In practice, this means prioritizing the well-being of our people, our country, and our planet over short-term political or personal gain. It means leading with aloha—compassion, love and understanding. It means standing with courage against the forces that thirst for war—in Congress, the propaganda media, the national security state, and the military-industrial complex.

This change in who we are as a nation, and in the leaders we choose to guide our country, will create a ripple effect that can transform our country and our world from one defined by conflict to one in which peace and prosperity are truly possible.

CHAPTER SIX
Fomenting Racism

The Democrat elite dishonor Rev. Martin Luther King Jr.'s dream by tearing us apart on the basis of the color of our skin, racializing everything, promoting segregation, and fomenting anti-white racism.

I was born on April 12, 1981, to a blue-eyed Caucasian mom from Michigan and a brown-skinned Polynesian dad from Samoa. Growing up in Hawaii, a melting pot of ethnicities and cultures from across the Pacific, Asia, and around the world, racial discrimination was not a part of my everyday life. While Hawaii is not some perfect utopia, by any measure, I'm grateful to have grown up with the culture and spirit of aloha, which is a recognition that we are all connected on a spiritual level as children of God. Living aloha inspires us to treat

143

others with love, respect, and compassion, regardless of race, ethnicity, social status, or any other superficial label.

Even with this upbringing, I was not naive about the vicious consequences of racism born from hating someone purely because of the color of their skin. As a kid, I read countless books about the horrors of slavery and found it inconceivable that people could be treated like animals and property because of their race. I admired the courage and heroism of people like Harriet Tubman, Rosa Parks, the Reverend Martin Luther King Jr., and so many others who put their lives on the line to fight against slavery, racism, and bigotry.

But it was one thing to read stories about heroes of the past; it was another thing to hear the stories my dad told us from his childhood as a brown-skinned Polynesian kid going to school in the Florida panhandle in 1955 when my grandfather was stationed at Eglin Air Force Base. Dad told us about his first day in his third grade class, when the teacher asked everyone to stand up and tell the class who they were and where they were from. My dad's turn came around and he said, "My name is Mike, I'm from Samoa." The teacher responded with, "Is that a country in Africa?" All of his classmates laughed at him. He was the only kid in the class who wasn't white. From that point on, he was teased and called "nigger boy," chased away from public water fountains and bathrooms that were marked "white only," and spat on as he walked down the street. He was confused—before Florida he had lived in Samoa, Hawaii, Massachusetts, and California as my Grandpa moved from one Air Force base to another. He had never been treated this way before.

In 1966, after graduating from high school, my dad started to hitch-hike from Florida to California with his guitar in hand, hoping to sing and play to cover his room and board along the way. After one ride, he was dropped off in Shreveport, Louisiana, on a sunny Sunday afternoon. He ended up stuck in the center of town for hours, wondering why no one would pick him up. Then, he saw a billboard across the street, with a picture of Martin Luther King Jr. under big letters that read: "MARTIN LUTHER KING AT COMMUNIST TRAINING SCHOOL." Someone had painted a red bullseye around King's face. Two years later, Martin Luther King Jr. was murdered in Tennessee.

Hearing my dad tell us what it was like for him growing up in the South shook me to my core. This wasn't a story I was reading in a book about a figure from the past who was no longer alive. This hit close to home. It was my dad—a guy who was born in American Samoa and ended up in the South because his dad served in the military. He was just a kid. He didn't know what was going on, or why it was "normal" for people with brown or black skin to be treated like second-class citizens at best, like animals at worst.

When I joined the Democrat Party over twenty years ago, this issue weighed heavy on my heart. I saw leaders in the party at that time who seemed to be committed to bringing the Reverend Martin Luther King's dream to life—a nation where we can be judged based on the content of our character rather than the color of our skin.

Sadly, today's Democrat elite have betrayed the memories, sacrifices, and dreams of leaders like Dr. Martin Luther King, reducing us to the color of our skin, using identity politics to tear us apart for their own political gain. They support programs teaching children they are born as either "the privileged" or "the victims," oppressors or oppressed—an immutable trait, they say, based solely on the color of their skin. They preach anti-racism, yet they have become the racists they claim to hate. I am no longer a Democrat because I could not stomach associating myself with those who, in their blind pursuit of power, defy Dr. King's dream, tear our country apart, foment racism, and fuel division.

Crossing the Bridge

In March 2019, I traveled with my former colleague Congressman John Lewis and other members of Congress to Selma, Alabama, on an annual pilgrimage organized by the Faith & Politics Institute. The mission of this trip was to bring people together—Democrats, Republicans, people of all backgrounds, ethnicities, and races—to walk in the footsteps of those who sacrificed so greatly during the Civil Rights Movement, draw inspiration from their example, and continue working toward a future where all Americans are treated equally and not judged by the color of their skin.

When I was vice chair of the Democratic National Committee, I was sitting in a nondescript hotel conference room, meeting with Democrat state party leaders from across the country. John Lewis was invited to share some words of encouragement with the group gathered there, and as he ended his remarks, he said with a slight smile and a chuckle, "Now go out there and make some good trouble." I smiled as he said that and wrote down his trademark phrase in my notebook. "Good trouble." If we are not making good trouble in the pursuit of having a positive impact in service to others and fixing what is broken in our society, are we really bringing about necessary change?

In the autumn of 1955, John Lewis, just fifteen years old, found himself listening to a young preacher named Martin Luther King Jr. on the radio. Immediately he knew he wanted to be a preacher just like the Reverend King. A few years later, he left his small hometown in Alabama and went on to become a leader of the Freedom Riders, a group of young people committed to peacefully protesting racial segregation. The group, which formed shortly after Rosa Parks was arrested for refusing to give up her seat on a bus to a white passenger, actively studied the tactics and methods of people like Mahatma Gandhi and Nelson Mandela, and how they brought about transformational change. The Freedom Riders were dedicated to their cause, and trained day and night, disciplined in their commitment to nonviolent protests, even in the face of the worst verbal and physical attacks.

As we sat on the bus traveling through Alabama, stopping at several historically significant sites of the Civil Rights Movement in Alabama, John Lewis and some of his fellow Freedom Riders shared firsthand accounts of what they experienced. We visited the old Woolworth's where John Lewis and his friends staged a sit-in—an establishment that had made it clear black people were not welcome. John talked about how they had trained for that protest, bringing in friends who acted as aggressors, yelling insults in their face, spitting at them, even physically assaulting them. The Freedom Riders sat and endured it all without making a sound or lifting a hand.

At a bus station in Rock Hill, South Carolina, a group of men beat John Lewis nearly to death before the police arrived, sent Lewis to jail, and let his assailants walk free. According to journalist David Remnick, Lewis "passed out the axioms of Jesus, Gandhi, Thoreau, and King to his fellow demonstrators even as he was being taunted as an agitator, a 'nigger,' a 'coon,' as teenaged thugs flicked lighted cigarettes at his neck. . . . Getting beaten, arrested, and jailed became a kind of routine, his regular service, and, after each incident, he would rest a little, as if all he had done was to put in a decent day's labor."[1]

Bloody Sunday

On March 7, 1965, the day began with a rally for voting rights—one of many that was held in Alabama during the first months of that year. In the days leading up to the rally Martin Luther King Jr. spoke at the funeral of a fellow civil rights activist, Jimmie Lee Jackson, who had been beaten, shot, and killed at a peaceful protest by a state trooper in Marion, Alabama. Martin Luther King Jr. encouraged the crowd—mourning and angered by the murder of their friend—saying,

"Jimmie Lee Jackson's death says to us that we must work passionately and unrelentingly to make the American dream a reality. His death must prove that unmerited suffering does not go unredeemed. We must not be bitter, and we must not harbor ideas of retaliating with violence. We must not lose faith in our white brothers."[2]

A few days later, about six hundred people, most of them black, lined up on one side of the Edmund Pettus Bridge, named after the last Confederate general to serve in the U.S. Senate, who was also the leader of the Alabama Ku Klux Klan. Their plan was to march more than fifty miles to the Alabama state capitol in Montgomery and demand that Governor George Wallace protect black Alabamans' right to vote. Wallace had gotten wind of this plan ahead of time, however, and declared that "a march cannot and will not be tolerated," adding that it was his duty to ensure "the protection of the lives and property of our citizens and those traveling through our state."[3]

Standing in Selma and staring across the bridge to the other side, John Lewis and his fellow marchers saw "a sea of blue-helmeted, blue-uniformed Alabama state troopers, line after line of them, dozens of battle-ready lawmen stretched from one side of U.S. Highway 80 to the other."[4]

The marchers stopped about fifty feet away from the state troopers. One of the troopers, Major John Cloud, shouted into a bullhorn: "It would be detrimental to your safety to continue this march. This is an unlawful assembly. You have to disperse, you are ordered to disperse. Go home or go to your church. This march will not continue."[5]

Sensing the danger that awaited them if they kept marching, John Lewis and Hosea Williams of the Southern Christian Leadership Conference attempted to reason with the officer. Williams said, "Mr. Major, I would like to have a word, can we have a word?"[6]

Cloud responded, "I've got nothing further to say to you," and gave the protestors two minutes to clear the bridge. John Lewis knelt on the ground and prayed. Hundreds of other marchers did the same. Writing in *Walking with the Wind*, he remembers "the clunk of the troopers' heavy boots, the whoops of rebel yells from the white onlookers, the clip-clop of horses' hooves hitting the hard asphalt of the highway, the voice of a woman shouting, 'Get 'em! *Get* the niggers!'"[7]

Most people would have turned and run. Not John Lewis. Grounded in his faith in God, he remained kneeling, as did nearly everyone who had come to march with him that day. And then, he writes, "they were upon us":

> The first of the troopers came over me, a large, husky man. Without a word, he swung his club against the left side of my head. I didn't feel any pain, just the thud of the blow, and my legs giving way. I raised an arm—a reflex motion—as I curled up in the "prayer for protection" position. And then the same trooper hit me again. And everything started to spin.
>
> I heard something that sounded like gunshots. And then a cloud of smoke rose all around us.
>
> Tear gas.
>
> I'd never experienced tear gas before. This, I would learn later, was a particularly toxic form called C-4, made to induce nausea.
>
> I began choking, coughing. I couldn't get air into my lungs. I felt as if I was taking my last breath. If there was ever a time in my life for me to panic, it should have been then. But I didn't. I remember how strangely calm I felt as I thought, this is it. People are going to die here. *I'm* going to die here.[8]

John suffered a skull fracture, retreating on wobbly legs to Brown Chapel. That night the nation was horrified to see the footage of what had happened on the Edmund Pettus Bridge. The brutality used against the Freedom Riders by law enforcement at the order of the governor shook Americans across the country out of their complacency.

The awakening that occurred that day, which became known as Bloody Sunday, made it possible for President Lyndon Johnson to win the support necessary to pass the Voting Rights Act of 1965. For years, similar legislation had been blocked by Southern Democrats in Congress. But after the events of Bloody Sunday, President Johnson, himself a Southern Democrat, stood up to members of his party and led the effort to ensure that all Americans, regardless of race, were respected and guaranteed their right to vote.

On March 25, 1965, less than three weeks after Bloody Sunday, Martin Luther King Jr., speaking from the steps of the state capitol in Montgomery, Alabama, declared that segregation was "on its deathbed":

> And so, I plead with you this afternoon as we go ahead: remain committed to nonviolence. Our aim must never be to defeat or humiliate the white man, but to win his friendship and understanding. We must come to see that the end we seek is a society at peace with itself, a society that can live with its conscience. And that will be a day not of the white man, not of the black man. That will be the day of man as man.
> I know you are asking today, "How long will it take?"....
> How long? Not long, because "no lie can live forever."....
> How long? Not long, because the arc of the moral universe is long, but it bends toward justice.[9]

As I stood on one side of the Edmund Pettus Bridge with John Lewis and a few dozen other members of Congress, I felt the gravity and weight of what those who had come before us endured. I was inspired by the courage and strength of character of those who had stood in this very spot and chosen to kneel in prayer to God instead of running away from their attackers and oppressors. A flood of emotion washed over me as we slowly began our walk across the bridge. It was an experience I will never forget. A hundred-plus people, walking arm in arm, honoring those who sacrificed their own well-being so others could walk free. Someone in the crowd started to sing, impromptu, "this little light of mine, I'm going to let it shine" and, one by one, people began joining in, until the vibration from over a hundred voices reverberated through the air.

As we walked across that bridge, I felt immense pride to live in a country where such transformational change had come about because of a courageous movement of peaceful protest and civil disobedience. I was struck not only by *what* the leaders of the Civil Rights Era had achieved, but *how* they had achieved it. They did not claim to have special rights; they asserted their equal rights. They did not denigrate the Founders of this nation or our founding documents; rather, they cited them in their defense. They did not claim that the United States was an irredeemable, hopeless place; instead, they dedicated their lives to make it better. They did not think America was defined by racism; they believed it was defined by its ideals—that all men are created equal and endowed by our Creator with unalienable rights. They chose to see the good in their fellow citizens. They knew that peaceful demonstrations would win more hearts and minds than violent riots ever could. In August 1963, in his famous "I Have a Dream" speech, Dr. King called the Declaration of Independence and the Constitution "a promissory note . . . to which every American was to fall heir. This note was a promise that all men—yes, Black men as well as white men—would be guaranteed the unalienable rights of life, liberty, and the pursuit of happiness."[10]

So-called progressives roll their eyes and summarily dismiss the sentiments that the Reverend King expressed. They see his dream as passé. They reject or ignore the truth that we are all children of God. They do not believe we are all created equal. They openly advocate for anti-white racism and insist that anyone who refuses to support their plan to turn Americans against one another is a racist himself. They believe we must judge each other by the color of our skin and segregate our society based on two classes: the oppressed (all people of color) and the oppressor (all white people). It is astounding and deeply disturbing to see these influential leaders in the Democrat Party betraying the Reverend Martin Luther King Jr.'s dream, fomenting divisiveness and discrimination and hate based on race. If things keep going on this way, we should not be surprised to see a rise in race-based violence in America.

They exalt people like professor Ibram X. Kendi, who claims that the United States is an irredeemably racist place where "the only remedy for past discrimination is present discrimination."[11] They tout writers like Ta-Nehisi Coates, who has said that "'White America' is a syndicate arrayed to protect its exclusive power to dominate and control our bodies," and called police and firefighters who served on 9/11 "menaces of nature."[12] They champion those who, under the guise of critical race theory, teach white kids in elementary school to feel guilty for being the oppressors that they are simply because of their race. The black students are taught to believe that they are inherently victims of racial oppression.

Walking Backward

Sometime in late 2018, I came across a paperback book called *White Fragility*. The book, which was written by an academic named Robin DiAngelo, summarized where the Democrat elite were headed, and the kind of racial transformation they were intent on exacting on our country.

What I read was deeply disturbing.

According to DiAngelo—who is a white woman—all white people are racist, and "anti-blackness is foundational" to white identity.[13] As DiAngelo says in the book, there is no way for white people to "fix themselves." She says, "a positive white identity is an impossible goal. White identity is inherently racist; white people do not exist outside the system of white supremacy."[14] The best a white person can hope to do, she explains, is to "strive to be 'less white," because "to be less white is to be less racially oppressive."[15]

When I read the book, I saw it for what it is—absolutely absurd. But the Democrat elite latched on to what she was selling and chose to use her work as a road map for restructuring America into a society where race is factored into every aspect of life. Self-serving Democrat politicians kicked Martin Luther King's dream to the curb to score cheap political points. They stand on their soapbox delivering speeches about "abolishing whiteness" and introduce bills that would make it legal to discriminate against white job applicants.

To them, nothing can be viewed in any way that *doesn't* involve race. Anyone who tries to take race out of the equation, or to look beyond it, is racist. To date, *White Fragility* has sold somewhere around 750,000 copies, and its author is raking in tens of thousands of dollars conducting "diversity seminars" at major American corporations, schools, and universities, using *White Fragility* as the primer.

During these seminars, employees of all races are forced to sit in a circle with Robin DiAngelo and listen to her repeat her hateful line that white people are inherently racist—and that there is absolutely nothing they can do about it. Anyone who dares to say this isn't true is told that their comments are only proof of their racism. Anyone who gets upset about being told they are racist is *especially* racist.[16]

Countless people have been forced by their bosses to sit through these highly divisive seminars and be subjected to this nonsense, in the name of diversity, equity, and inclusion (DEI).

This is the hypocrisy: to speak of *any other race* in the way that DiAngelo writes about white people would be cause for immediate cancellation and social censure. But since DiAngelo is talking about white people—the only group in the United States against whom racism is not only permissible, it is *encouraged*, or even *required*—she is getting away with it and making big bucks from it.

In his book *How to Be an Antiracist*, Ibram X. Kendi claims that there is no such thing as a person who is simply "not racist." Either people are racists—which Kendi assures us is the case for most people—or they are "antiracist." Kendi says that "the only remedy for past discrimination is present discrimination"—in other words, racism is the only remedy for racism.[17]

This has become the doctrine of today's Democrat elite, in politics and the propaganda media; and the consequences are dangerous. Not only are they openly promoting racism, they have drastically lowered the bar for what justifies calling someone "racist," thereby cheapening the seriousness of a charge of racism and hurting those who are victims of actual racism.

Robin DiAngelo sets the bar so low that all a person must do is *be white* for one to be assumed a racist. To her, and her followers, nothing matters than the color of one's skin. Those with white skin are not allowed to defend themselves. Anyone who *isn't* white, however, can talk endlessly about the various ways they have been victimized by the omnipresent white supremacy they say emanates from all white people, no matter who they are.

This kind of victimhood playacting—pretending to be the victim of racism, because it's cool and it might advance your career in academia, HR, politics, or the arts—is an insult to the memory and immeasurable sacrifice of men like Martin Luther King Jr., who put his life on the line so we could live in a society where all people are treated as individuals, and judged not by the color of our skin, but by the content of our character. He strove to *end* the practice of making broad generalizations where rewards and punishments, legal status, and civil rights are designated based on race. It didn't matter whether the group being attacked was white, black, or something else. He fought for this because he knew better than anyone what it was like to be judged based on nothing but one's skin color.

The Bottom Line

We cannot allow the Democrat elite to continue to foment hatred and racism in America, tearing us apart and unraveling the great progress that has been made, as a direct result of the sacrifices of leaders like John Lewis and the Reverend Martin Luther King Jr.

Much damage has been done, but all hope is not lost. Every one of us, as Americans, has the power, responsibility, and opportunity to stop this insanity and come together as one nation, under God, and bring about the future that the Reverend King envisioned for us all.

He visited Hawaii just three weeks after it achieved statehood in 1959 and, during his visit, spoke to the Hawaii State Legislature. Recognizing the power of the aloha spirit he felt in Hawaii, he said, "I come to you with a great deal of appreciation and great feeling of appreciation." Dr. King went on to say that Hawaii served as a "noble example" of what was possible in terms of "racial harmony and racial justice"—of what was possible even in the South, where the "struggle" was still ongoing.[18]

After returning to the mainland, King shared his experiences in Hawaii with his congregation, saying, "As I looked at all of these various faces and various colors mingled together like the waters of the sea, I could see only one face—the face of the future!"

If we wish to fulfill the dream that Martin Luther King Jr. and other heroes of the Civil Rights Movement described in such beautiful detail to us in the 1960s, we must truly take to heart the truth that is the foundation of King's message and that is enshrined in the Preamble to the Declaration of Independence: *"We hold these truths to be self-evident, that all men are created equal, that they are endowed by their Creator with certain unalienable Rights, that among these are Life, Liberty and the pursuit of Happiness."*

Whether you believe in God or not, the truth remains: we are not the color of our skin, or our ethnicity, or any other superficial designation. Our true identity is that we are all children of God, eternal spiritual beings, only temporarily in a material body, for a very short period of time. When the body dies, we do not die.

The root cause of racism is hatred based on mistakenly identifying someone as the color of their skin. When we know and accept the truth that our bodies are temporary, and not who we really are, judging someone based on their race is as crazy as judging someone because of the color of their shirt.

To truly defeat the ignorance, hatred, and bigotry that fuel racism, we must follow Dr. King's example, respond to hatred with aloha—love and compassion—and share with others the truth about our true spiritual identity, who we really are. Responding to hate with more hate feeds into the darkness of evil that led to slavery, lynching, and segregation.

If we sincerely want to end the cycle of racism and hatred in our society, we must draw inspiration from the example of Dr. King, John Lewis, and the Freedom Riders who responded to extreme hatred, racism, and violence with peaceful protest, love, and a positive vision for what is possible when we truly live aloha.

This isn't always easy to do. We cannot do it on our own. We find strength and inspiration in God's unconditional and eternal love for every one of us, and share that love with others to defeat the forces of darkness, hatred, and bigotry.

Martin Luther King Jr. closed his remarks to the Hawaii Legislature with the words of a prayer by "an old Negro slave preacher:" "Lord, we ain't what we want to be; we ain't what we ought to be; we ain't what we gonna be, but thank God, we ain't what we was."

There is still work to be done to bring the Reverend Dr. King's dream to life. We must learn from our past and honor the heroic sacrifices of those who fought for the great progress that has been realized in our country. We must stand together to defeat the darkness of racism and hate being propagated by self-serving politicians, so-called progressives, and their allies in the mainstream media. We defeat that darkness with love—by treating each other with aloha, seeing past our superficial colors and clothes, and respecting each other for who we really are: children of God.

CHAPTER SEVEN

What's True? The Powerful Decide

The Democrat elite deny the existence of objective truth and the biological differences between men and women. In the ultimate expression of hatred and hostility toward women, and our Creator, they are trying to "erase" our existence altogether.

The Truth

When I think back to my childhood, and some of the earliest lessons I learned, there were certain things I just knew to be true. The sky is blue. Boiling water is hot. The ocean is salty. When I go in the water, I get wet. If I stand in the sun, I will dry. Without knowing the science of gravity, I knew that when something dropped from my hands, it would fall to the ground. I also knew, without a doubt, the difference between boys and girls. The kids I grew up with came in all different shapes, colors, and sizes, but I was never confused about their sex. I have three older brothers, two of whom went through a long-hair phase. I went through a major tomboy phase. I thought dolls and makeup were boring and lame. I had a short boy's haircut, wore surf shorts and T-shirts every day, spent many afternoons practicing martial arts, kicking trees, and running up mountains barefoot because I knew it would make me stronger and tough. Never once did I think my brothers were actually girls or that I was actually a boy. As time went on, I grew out of that phase, and my brothers cut their hair (making our mom very happy) while I grew mine out. I still practice martial arts but am happy to dress up every now and then. Regardless of any external expression or feeling, the objective truth of our biological sex was never in question.

It is shocking to me that in just a few short years, we went from a near universal acceptance of the fact that there are biological differences between men and women, to now living in a world where the Democrat elite are actively rejecting biological facts. Through their denial of biological differences between men and women, and claiming that anyone, at any time, can become a woman simply by stating that they feel like a woman, the Democrat elite are denying the existence of objective truth. By doing this, they are eliminating the foundation of civilized society.

They are so blinded by their arrogance and desire to be God that they believe they can author truth or reality. Being so deluded, they truly believe (and want us to believe) that we must reject even the most obvious truths—such as that the male body is biologically different and distinct from the female body. If they can deceive themselves and the rest of us on this most fundamental and obvious truth, then they can convince themselves and us of anything. Black is white, white is black, up is down, down is up, and a wide-open border is closed. What's bad for us is good; what's good for us is bad. There are no limits. I cannot associate myself with a political party that so easily rejects the existence of truth just to score some political power points. If they are willing to sacrifice truth, there are no boundaries and nothing is sacred.

The Courage to Speak

Growing up in Gallatin, Tennessee, Riley Gaines spent hours swimming in her parents' pool, dreaming of breaking Olympic swimming records. Her hard work paid off and before long she was swimming at the University of Kentucky where, as a standout scholar athlete, she qualified for U.S. Olympic team trials in 2021.

But Riley and her fellow female swimmers soon had unexpected and unwelcome competition—from a biological man who called himself Lia Thomas. Lia Thomas had been formerly known as William Thomas, a male swimmer at the University of Pennsylvania, where he was ranked as the 462nd best swimmer in the country.[1] Once Thomas declared that he was a "woman" and started competing against female swimmers, he suddenly began winning major competitions. It came at a cost. Unfairly forced to compete against a biological male with a clear physical advantage, many women saw their hopes of national championship victories and Olympic trials go out the window. They were forced to share a locker room with Thomas, showering and changing in front of a biological male who at times was visibly sexually aroused in front of them, and who bragged to them about his sexual exploits with women.

When these young women complained to their school administrators, teachers, the NCAA, and the Ivy League school which Thomas represented, no one cared. They showed no sympathy or empathy for the plight of these young women. Their concern was reserved solely for the man who called himself Lia Thomas, bending over backward to accommodate him.

In the 2022 NCAA championships, Lia Thomas and Riley Gaines tied for fifth place in the two-hundred-yard freestyle. Since the judge didn't have two trophies, he decided to give the one he had to Lia Thomas. Riley asked the judge why Thomas deserved the trophy over her, and after making a few weak excuses, the judge finally admitted that it was just easier this way and that he'd send Riley her trophy in the mail. For her, it wasn't about the trophy at all; she had a shelf full of them at home. Riley knew what was happening was wrong. She didn't understand how these judges and administrators so easily dismissed objective reality. Why was this man suddenly able to compete against women? There are obvious biological advantages for a male swimmer competing in an all-female competition, which is why most sports have separate competitions based on biological sex. Bone density, muscle mass, and testosterone levels give men undeniable advantages in strength, speed, and endurance. According to a study published in 2021 by the *British Journal of Sports Medicine*, even two years after hormone therapy, men who had "transitioned" into "transgender women" still had a significant advantage in strength and speed over biological women.[2] In many athletic competitions, the margins of victory can be very small. In swimming or sprinting, fractions of a second can be the difference between first place, second place, third place, or not qualifying at all. Most biological males start with physical advantages that no biological woman will ever be able to match, no matter how hard she might train.

Riley could have easily moved on with her life after graduating from college. Instead, she chose to fight for truth and fairness for female athletes. Unsurprisingly, the so-called "woke" mob turned their sights on Riley and began their assault. They can't allow the truth to be heard because their insanity is exposed. So they try to drown out the truth with verbal and physical assaults. When Riley is giving a speech where she shares her personal story, there is almost always someone in the crowd booing or yelling insults. Protestors picket outside. After she spoke at San Francisco State University on April 6, 2023 on the topic of "Saving Women's Sports," Riley was told by university security that it would be unsafe for her to leave the classroom where she spoke because protestors had entered the building and were headed her way. The mob gathered in the hallway, screaming insults and making violent threats. When Riley finally left, with the assistance of security guards and police officers, protestors tried to block her path, screaming nasty insults in her face, and a man dressed in a woman's dress punched her.

Still, Riley is not deterred. She said to Tucker Carlson in a recent interview, "When they want me to be silenced, it just means I need to speak louder."

Riley and her teammates are not alone in their experiences. Bethany Hamilton, a competitive female surfer who overcame great adversity after she lost her left arm to a shark attack at age thirteen, spoke out when the World Surf League made the controversial decision to allow biological males who identify as women to compete against women on tour, as long as they had been taking testosterone for twelve months. Hamilton posted a very respectful and thoughtful video on social media explaining why this was a bad idea, and suggesting the WSL should create a separate division in surfing for those who identify as trans. She said that until the WSL changes their policy, she would boycott the WSL. She later put out a tweet saying, "Male-bodied athletes should not be competing in female sports. Period."[3] The backlash began. Her decades-long sponsor Rip Curl dropped their sponsorship of her. On International Women's Day, it is customary that male surfers competing on the WSL tour wear the name of a woman they admire on their jersey. In previous years, Hamilton's name was one that surfers chose to wear because of her incredible and inspiring story. However, in 2023, surfers who wanted to wear her name on their jersey were told by WSL officials that they couldn't because "she doesn't support the WSL and she doesn't support equality."[4, 5]

Biological males competing against, and beating, females in sports is becoming more commonplace. Often, these are boys or men who are not doing well competing in the male division, so they simply grow out their hair and declare they are female, compete against girls and do very well, and often, win. Recently, a male sophomore with long hair in New Hampshire won a girl's high school state title with a jump of 5'2". In the boys' division, the winning jump was 6' and the lowest boys' jump was 5'6".[6]

Martina Navratilova, retired tennis champion and one of the greatest athletes of all time, posted on X, "And I will keep saying this as [sic] nauseum until the rules change- women's sports are not a place for failed athletes."[7] Navratilova, one of the greatest tennis players of all time, has been outspoken on this issue for years, speaking very candidly about how unfair it is to women to face biological males in sports.

This is happening in girls and women's sports across the country and around the world. Scholarships are being lost and opportunities to compete at the highest levels are going away, because of the unfairness of allowing biological men to compete in women's sports.

Whether we realize it or not, this is an issue that impacts us all. This problem is only getting worse, not going away. Unless we take action, this infection of insanity and rejection of objective truth will continue to spread.

The Miss Universe pageant changed its rules in 2012 to allow men to compete. When I saw this, I thought, *This is strange, isn't there a Mr. Universe pageant?* Yes, of course, there is. Yet, in 2023, two male competitors representing the Netherlands and Portugal competed at the international Miss Universe pageant. Rikkie Valerie Kollé of the Netherlands said, "as a little boy I conquered all the things that came through my path—and look at me now, standing here as a strong, empowering and confident trans woman."[8]

In 2022, *USA Today* named Richard/Rachel Levine one of its 2022 Women of the Year. Minnesota State Representative Leigh Finke, a man identifying as a woman, is one of *USA Today*'s 2023 Women of the Year. *Time Magazine* selected MJ Rodriguez, a biological male, as one of their 2022 Women of the Year. The list goes on.

For those who dare to call out this insanity for what it is, we are attacked and canceled, and in some places even risk being charged with a crime. The UK's Labour Party is advocating for "mis-gendering" someone to be a crime punishable with a possible two-year prison sentence.[9]

Under the Biden-Harris administration, the federal Equal Employment Opportunity Commission issued guidance stating that "the intentional and repeated use of a name or pronoun inconsistent with the individual's gender identity . . . will constitute actionable sex harassment."

These are all symptoms of the insanity that results from a rejection of objective truth. To make things worse, it's not enough to just live and let live, agree to disagree. Those who are propagating this nonsense are trying to force the rest of us to comply and in the process sacrifice something as fundamental as freedom of speech.

On the Basis of Sex

The irony is that the Democrat Party has long touted itself as the party that champions women's rights and equality. It still does. It was Democrats in Congress who led the charge to pass a law that is now commonly known as Title IX. The law consists of a single, direct sentence containing only thirty-seven words:

**No person in the United States shall, on the basis of sex, be
excluded from participation in, be denied the benefits of, or
be subjected to discrimination under any education program
or activity receiving Federal financial assistance.**[10]

The language is very clear. You don't have to be a lawyer or a
professor to understand this law or appreciate why it was passed.
At the time Title IX was written, colleges that had admitted only
men—including many Ivy League schools—were beginning to open
their doors to women, and many were taking advantage of the opportunity. According to R. Shep Melnick, the author of *The Transformation
of Title IX*, when the law was enacted, "only 15 percent of college
varsity athletes were women; four decades later that proportion was 43
percent. Between 1972 and 2015 the number of female varsity athletes
at National Collegiate Athletic Association Schools increased sevenfold.
At the high school level female participation is now ten times what it
was in 1970, rising from less than 300,000 to over 3 million. In 1970
only 7 percent of interscholastic athletes were female. Today that number is 42 percent."[11]

For many years after the passage of Title IX, the Democrat Party
touted these statistics that proved Title IX to be so effective. However,
today's Democrat elite have revealed that they really don't care about
women at all. In their pursuit of power, and fear of angering the small
but very vocal trans community, the Biden-Harris administration and
Democrat elite are trying to erase women by denying the biological
and objective truth that a man is a man and a woman is a woman.
They have wholeheartedly embraced the falsehood that any man can
become a woman if he believes he's a woman, and vice versa. No
questions asked. When Congressman Mark Takano, a Democrat
from California, was asked in a Congressional hearing, if Mike Tyson
declared today that he is now a woman, should he be allowed to

compete against women boxers, Takano replied, without hesitation, "Yes."[12]

I was speechless for a moment when I saw the video of this exchange. Did he say yes because he really believes Mike Tyson would become a woman simply by declaring that to be the reality? Or did he say yes because he was too afraid to say the truth? There is no logic that can explain this insanity. What is crystal clear is that Democrats like Congressman Takano do not care about women at all, or in this case, the physical harm that would befall female boxers if they were forced to compete against male boxers like Tyson.

Not only do they not care, they apparently don't know what a woman is. During the Supreme Court confirmation hearings for Judge Ketanji Brown Jackson, Senator Marsha Blackburn asked Judge Jackson to define the word "woman." Judge Jackson said she couldn't answer the question because she is "not a biologist."[13] Other senators attempted to get Judge Jackson to define the word, and they were all met with similar obfuscation. Yet, this was a person asking to be confirmed for a job on the Supreme Court where she would have to make decisions based on the biological differences between men and women. How can we place our trust in the judgment of a person who rejects one of the most objective facts: that there are biological differences between a man and a woman? We can't.

In what is the height of hatred and hostility toward women, the Democrat elite are trying to erase women altogether by changing our language and getting rid of different versions of the word "woman." In May 2022, Democrats in Congress introduced abortion legislation where instead of the word "woman," they used "person," claiming that the new language was more inclusive because according to them, men can now get pregnant.

A few months later, the National Education Association, the country's largest labor union, proposed a rule that would ban the word "mother," replacing it with "birthing parent."[14] One year earlier, the Biden administration had released its annual budget, which replaced the phrase "pregnant women" with "birthing people."[15]

In an interview with Anderson Cooper on CNN, Representative Alexandria Ocasio-Cortez referred to women as "menstruating persons."[16] Other Democrats are using the term "birthing people" instead of "women" and "chestfeeders" rather than women who breastfeed.[17]

In July 2022, during a Senate Judiciary Committee, Senator Josh Hawley attempted to clarify a statement made by University of California, Berkeley, law professor Khiara M. Bridges during her testimony. She said, "Many women, cis women, have the capacity for pregnancy. Many cis women do not have the capacity for pregnancy. There are also trans men who are capable of pregnancy as well as non-binary people who are capable of pregnancy."[18] When Senator Hawley suggested that given that definition, this issue might not truly be a "women's rights" issue, Professor Bridges interrupted him several times claiming his line of questioning was "transphobic," that it "opens up trans people to violence by not recognizing them."[19]

In 2022, President Biden and his administration chose to mark the fiftieth anniversary of Title IX's passage by quietly bypassing Congress and using the bureaucratic state to change the definition of Title IX so that it includes "gender identity." They threatened to punish schools that limit women's sports to biological females by taking away funding for meals for children who can't afford to buy school lunches.[20]

Anticipating the Biden administration may try to pull this kind of dishonest and unconstitutional stunt, in 2020 I introduced a bipartisan bill in Congress called the Protect Women's Sports Act. This bill very simply clarified that the historic Title IX protections are based on biological sex, reflecting the intent of those who originally crafted and fought for the passage of Title IX. Allowing biological males to compete against biological women and girls in sports directly undermines the intent of Title IX.

As expected, I immediately received a barrage of vicious attacks from activist groups, Democrats in Congress, the mainstream propaganda media, and trolls online. I was called all the names you might expect. "Transphobe." "Bigot." "Hate-monger." "TERF" (trans-exclusionary radical feminist). "Sexist." "Racist." And worse.

None of those who attacked me and called me names were willing to stop for a moment to appreciate the hypocrisy and insanity of their rejection of objective truth. Not one of them was willing to acknowledge that their position was anti-woman, undermining Title IX and causing harm to women and girls across America. Stating the fact that there are biological differences between males and females, and creating competitive rules that acknowledge that fact, does not stop those who identify as "transgender" from forming their own divisions to compete in sports or pageants. Their rights are not being denied.

Given the extreme backlash and vitriol that crashes down like an avalanche on anyone who dares to say, "There is such a thing as a woman," I understand why many people are afraid to speak up. They may be concerned they will lose their job, or a school scholarship, or have family and friends who turn their backs on them. Even though it may be hard or even frightening, now is *not* the time to put our heads in the sand or cower in the corner. There is too much at stake.

The Bottom Line

The most common response from the Democrat elite when this is brought up is to say, this is not a real problem. "Stop overblowing this issue; only a few people are impacted by this," they say. But they're wrong—both about how many young girls and women are impacted by this and about the corrosive effect their actions and policies are having on our country. This issue reaches far beyond college scholarships or losing a beauty pageant.

The underlying issue here is the Democrat elite's rejection of objective truth. This affects us all in a very serious way. They are removing the guardrails of what is objectively and fundamentally true or false, and attempting to put themselves in the position to be the sole authority to dictate truth and lies, information and disinformation. When those guardrails are removed, anything goes. There is no such thing as right and wrong, true or false. Those in power believe they, and they alone, should play God, dictating what is true and right, and that we must all bend the knee and accept whatever they declare to be true without question, challenge, or dissent. If we do not comply, we are certain to face their wrath and punishment. This is not a theory. This is happening now, and we are seeing the negative effects on our society. We are being threatened if we use the wrong language. Expressing our opinion or views that are different from the Democrat elite sanctioned position is cause for cancellation, censorship, or smears. The concept of a respectful, open discussion about what is happening in our country is no longer welcome or allowed in most places.

If we are to have any hope of living free in America and raising our children to be critical thinkers with the freedom to exercise their own judgment based on facts, we cannot allow this to continue. We cannot stand silently by and accept their insanity. We can't just go along to get along.

We must raise our voices to speak the truth and have the courage of the child who calls out, "The Emperor has no clothes!" We must use our votes and our influence to reject the insanity of today's Democrat elite who do not care about the truth, reality, or the well-being and interests of the American people. They are dangerous because they're motivated by fear of losing power and are willing to do anything and everything to retain that power. They cannot be trusted and should not be in power.

CHAPTER EIGHT

Families Under Fire

Today's Democrat elite are undermining our families, declaring that "the state"—rather than parents—knows what's best for children.

The Democrat establishment, in its endless pursuit of power, is undermining the bedrock institution of the family and have declared that they know better than parents what is best for children. Their policies and actions consistently advance the interests of the state at the cost of what's best for families, children, and our society.

These elitists ridicule and fight against the freedom of parents to choose where their child goes to school. They indoctrinate our children from a very young age with their narrative about systemic racism, what pronouns to use, sexual orientation, and transgender ideology. They are playing the long game, inculcating their so-called progressive agenda into our children when they're very young, and discouraging any real challenge, questions, or critical thought. They encourage children to pursue irreversible hormone treatment and surgeries in the name of "gender-affirming care," often without the knowledge of the child's parents. When parents object to any of this, at a minimum they are ridiculed on social media, rebuked by the schools and teachers' unions, threatened that their child may be forcibly removed from their care, and sometimes even targeted as "domestic terrorists" by the Biden administration.

I can no longer associate myself with a political party who, at every turn, is undermining the family—the very foundation of our civilization—and callously sacrificing the well-being of our children and families to advance their woke political agenda.

Woke Agenda vs. Education

By any measure, my own education path was a little different from the norm. I was homeschooled through high school, and absolutely loved it. I was able to go at my own pace, spending more time on the subjects that required it, and speeding through subjects where I excelled. My parents are entrepreneurs and longtime small business owners, so part of my learning experience was helping my dad tally up the sales receipts for the day, balancing the books, and applying math lessons to real-world problems. A strong work ethic came from all five of us kids working in our family restaurant—my brothers as dishwashers, cashiers, and servers, and my sister and I wiping counters, clearing tables, sweeping and mopping floors, and most importantly, welcoming customers like they were part of our family. We were on a first-name basis with our regulars, many of whom came in and ate lunch and dinner with us. I learned how to type when I was ten years old through a Typing Tutor game on an old MS-DOS computer that had the basic green letters on a black screen, and helped my parents by transcribing letters and memos for them.

I could go on and on. I loved that my education was not limited to what was in a textbook; it was informed by real-world experiences. I give my parents great credit for deciding to raise us this way, especially at a time when homeschooling was rare and looked down upon. We weren't allowed to leave the house until after 2 p.m. out of concern we might get picked up by police for truancy. There weren't very many resources available to homeschooling families, but my parents persevered anyway. They decided early on that they weren't going to cede the serious responsibility of our education, especially during our most formative years, to a stranger. They wanted to set us up for success with a strong foundation of values, critical and independent thinking, and a problem-solving mindset. I'm so grateful to them for doing this, even though at the time I didn't fully understand the impact it would have on my life. In hindsight, I realize how prescient they were, already seeing red flags that pointed to a broken education system seeking to indoctrinate children with a certain value set that may or may not be aligned with the values my parents wanted to instill in us.

In today's schools, the fundamentals of reading, writing, math, and science are an afterthought. This is not the fault of teachers. They are micromanaged and extremely restricted in what they can and can't do, and they don't get to choose what curriculum they teach from. Often, they are forced to teach to a test or a certain curriculum that was created by someone else far away who has no idea what their students might really need. I have so much admiration for those who step up and have a heart for teaching, even though they know going in how challenging it can be, how little they will be paid, and most importantly, what an important task they've been charged with.

It is really the teachers' unions and politicians who run the show, and unfortunately, they don't seem to care much about our kids getting a good education. Their top priorities are self-preservation and finding ways to amass more power.

When I was campaigning during the 2020 presidential primary, I visited rural communities across the country, many stricken with poverty. One of the most common issues raised to me by parents was how terrible the public school system was, and how they wish they had other options. They wanted the right to choose where and how to educate their child—whether it be at a charter school, special skills school, religious school, a school outside their neighborhood, or getting support to school their children at home. A poll conducted in June 2023 by RealClear Opinion found that 71 percent of Americans support school choice, with a majority of both Democrat and Republican support, and including 70 percent of Asian, 73 percent of Black, 71 percent of Hispanic, and 71 percent of White voters.[1] This majority continues to increase over time. Why haven't Democrat politicians picked up on this growing demand for school choice? They will not support school choice because the teacher union bosses will not allow it.

Randi Weingarten, the head of the nation's largest teacher union, said that school choice "undermines democracy." Wow, that escalated quickly. How does providing parents the freedom to choose what education is best for their children undermine democracy, one might ask? Randi says school choice is about "undermining democracy and undermining civil discourse and undermining pluralism because 90% of our kids go to public schools still," she said. "They just divide. Divide. Divide. Divide."[2]

The main argument that unions use against school choice is that it defunds public schools, and that taxpayer dollars should instead go toward running public schools and hiring more teachers. There are several problems with their argument. First and foremost, taxpayer dollars designated for education should actually go toward educating our children in the way that is best for them. Every child is unique, with different abilities, skills, and learning styles. Taking a cookie-cutter approach to education, as we have seen, doesn't work very well. By implementing things like school vouchers, parents have the freedom to choose where to send their child to school, and schools are incentivized to improve the quality of education so parents will choose to send their kids to those schools.

Second, even if you buy into their funding argument, the statistics tell us that our public school system, overall, is failing our children. In 2023, according to the U.S. Department of Education, around 130 million Americans read at less than a sixth grade level. That's more than 50 percent of adults in our country.[3] 21 percent of adults—32 million people—in America cannot read at all. One in four children in America grows up without learning how to read.[4] Even among the top ten states with the highest numbers of children's reading proficiency, the average percentage of students with low reading proficiency is 55 percent.

The union bosses and Democrat elite pretend to care about the well-being of impoverished, low-income, and minority children, and argue that school choice would hurt them most. It's hard to believe them when the reality is, like most wealthy people, union leaders and politicians already have school choice—they can afford to send their children to the best private schools. Yet, they earn their livelihood depriving parents who don't have much money from having that same freedom. CNN Primetime host Abby Phillips confronted Chicago Teachers Union president Stacy Davis Gates about how she could so strongly oppose school choice while sending her own son to a private school. Phillips said, "You've likened in the past private schools of today to quote 'segregation academies' of the Jim Crow South. Why then send your child to a private school after speaking out so publicly against them?" Davis Gates replied, "I didn't speak out against private schools. I spoke out against school choice. School choice and private schools are two different entities."[5] Abby Phillips pressed on, saying,

"You wrote that to explain why you chose to take your child out of public school for a sports program at a private school," she said. "The question I think your critics are asking is why not afford that nuance to the families who might live in the South Side of Chicago and in other major cities, and they want the same choice that you were able to afford to give to your child?" Davis Gates continued to sidestep the direct question Phillips asked of her, leading Phillips to conclude, "I also think that what you just described for your son is choice that you made for your family, and I think that's what your critics are pointing out here."

Kudos to Abby Phillips for pointing out the obvious hypocrisy that is prolific among school choice opponents.

Please don't misunderstand—there is an important distinction to be made here. I have great admiration for teachers. While my parents are entrepreneurs at heart, they are both teachers by trade whose first jobs after college were as educators in American Samoa. My father-in-law recently retired after twenty years of being a public school teacher. I have walked the picket line with teachers on strike, demanding better pay and support for them so they can focus on their critical mission of educating our children. Most teachers want what's best for our kids and are frustrated to no end at the many obstacles that inhibit their ability to provide kids with the education they need and deserve.

The problem here are the Democrat elite, which include teachers' union bosses, who aren't motivated by a desire to improve our kids' education, but are instead focused on gaining more power and pushing their so-called progressive value system on our kids.

They should be waking up every day eager to take on the challenge of making sure every child in America excels in reading, writing, math, and science, and has an appreciation and understanding of our country's history, our Constitution and Bill of Rights, and the vision our nation's Founders had for America. They should recognize their foremost responsibility is to educate, and leave the raising of children to parents who will instill their own set of values in their kids.

Instead, the Democrat elite are taking it upon themselves to do this, starting with the teaching of things like critical race theory in elementary school, which, in essence, teaches that racism is inherently a part of American society. Adults can debate about critical race theory in a college classroom or public forum, but it is completely inappropriate and damaging to mandate it be taught to young children in school. In the name of critical race theory, white children are taught they have "white privilege" and are the oppressor, no matter who are they are, and black children are inherently victims and the oppressed. This kind of mass judgment of a person based on their skin color, or some other superficial association, is wrong and dangerous. This kind of thought, taken to the most extreme level, is the kind of thing that drove Hitler's evil Holocaust. It is what was behind the indefensible crime of slavery, and the violence, discrimination, and oppression that followed. It is important that our children learn the whole truth about our country's history, which includes the worst parts about our nation's past. Along with that, however, we must also teach and apply the lessons learned from this past, foremost of which is that racism does not defeat racism, discrimination does not defeat discrimination. We must stop the insanity of judging and discriminating against an entire group of people on the basis of race, ethnicity, political affiliation, or other superficial designation. Instead, treat each other with respect, as children of God and fellow Americans, and judge people on the content of their character.

Parents vs. the Government

One of the most troubling elements of the Democrat elite's agenda is the sexualization of young children at the hands of so-called progressive teachers, administrators, and politicians. At a time when our kids are supposed to be able to enjoy their innocence and childhood—running around outside, playing pretend, and arguing over whether Godzilla or King Kong would win in a fight—they are instead being asked questions about their gender identities and forced to decide what their sexualities are. They're doing this through children's TV shows and books written specifically for young kids.

When I first heard about these inappropriate, lewd books and shows, it was from concerned parents doing interviews on cable news expressing their outrage and sincere worry. In those short interviews, usually the host or another guest scoffed at the parents' concerns, saying that the parents need to calm down and stop exaggerating the issue. As usual, that was when the interview was cut off—before the concerned parent could respond.

I met some of these parents when I was invited to speak to a group called Parents Defending Education in Virginia shortly after the 2021 Virginia gubernatorial election. This election made national news because of the shocking defeat of the Democrat establishment and longtime Clintonite Terry McAuliffe who, according to the political pundits, was supposed to win that race. About six weeks before the election, Larry Sabato, the director of the University of Virginia Center for Politics, summed up the attitude of Democrats in the state: "Oh, we'll win in the end, we always do, it's a blue state."[6] That was before McAuliffe said in a debate in late September, "I don't think parents should be telling schools what they should teach,"[7] in response to ongoing disputes and protests organized by parents at Board of Education meetings regarding highly sexualized books in elementary schools.

Parents and families across party lines were outraged by McAuliffe's statement, and didn't fall for his attempt to retract his statement. They knew he said it because he believed it. It was a major turning point in the election that motivated people to make their voices heard, regardless of partisan politics. Shocking the Washington establishment, McAuliffe was defeated in that election, and the Republican candidate, Glenn Youngkin, overcame a double-digit deficit in the polls to win by 3 percent.

I met with the parents who led this effort across Virginia, just a few days after the election, and the energy in the room was electric. There were parents from across the country who flew in for this meeting, inspired by the difference Virginia parents made. They lifted up their voices, came together, and brought about change, not based on partisan politics but, rather, around what is best for their children, their families, and society. They changed the outcome of an election that many professional political pundits said was a fait accompli. They defeated the candidate who felt that the government knows what's best for children more than parents do.

After our meeting, a few of the group's leaders pulled me aside to talk about how their plans to extend their efforts nationwide, and support parents reaching out to them from across the country asking for advice and help. As we talked, I noticed a stack of books on the table. These were many of the same books I had seen them hold up in interviews. I grabbed one of the books, *Gender Queer*, a memoir written by Maia Kobabe, a person who uses e/em/eir pronouns, and started flipping through the pages. I couldn't believe my eyes. The drawings and pictures in the book were some of the most twisted, graphic sexual images I'd ever seen. It was extremely inappropriate for elementary and middle schoolers, who were the target audience for this book. It's no wonder these parents were incensed by school boards and administrators who had the audacity to push this obscene content in front of their kids. They would not let this stand. Parents Defending Action has grown into a national support and advocacy group for parents across the country who are waking up to the reality of what's going on and taking action to protect their children.

Another issue parents are growing increasingly alarmed about is news that teachers in many schools are being told they're not allowed to inform parents if their child decides to identify as a different gender. Parents are left completely in the dark. This happened to one of my father-in-law's students. This student named Scott announced in class that he now identified as a girl and wanted to be called Sarah.[8] Naturally, my father-in-law's first instinct was to talk to the child's parents, keep them informed, and make sure the child was getting the care and support that he needed. So my father-in-law went to the principal and told him about his plan. He was immediately shut down and told that under no circumstances would he have any conversation or communication with the student's parents on this matter. This was school policy. There was no way around it. In some cases, this goes even further—the schools go behind parents' backs and help children get prescriptions for hormone blockers, and find doctors who will help them begin an irreversible and harmful process of chemical castration and surgeries—all without parental notification or consent. They justify their actions in the name of providing "gender-affirming care," even though they ultimately end up harming the child who is not at all equipped to make a life-changing decision.

Sadly, this is not a fringe issue. Contrary to the talking point most often used by the Democrat elite, it doesn't affect just a few people. It cannot be easily dismissed. The reality is that people in whom parents place their trust—teachers and doctors—are among those cooperating with the so-called progressive agenda to confuse and mislead young people. For teachers, the incentives might be ideological, given how strongly the teachers' unions are pushing this. For doctors, the incentives might be financial, given how profitable "gender-affirming care" can be. But in both cases, they are rejecting objective truth and peddling the pernicious lie that one's sex (or "gender") is a subjective matter, based on personal feelings, or a "social construct." Not only is this a lie, but, as we well know, feelings can change, even more so with young children.

Parents, meanwhile, are told that unless they support putting their daughters on puberty blockers, suppressing their hormones, and go along with cruel and unnecessary mastectomies (which are now called "top surgeries" to make it sound less scary), they will face serious consequences. First, there is social ostracization. Then, parents are warned that if they stand in the way of their children receiving mastectomies, castration, or other irreversible surgeries, they will likely lose their child to suicide. Now, in some cases, the government is threatening to take children away from parents who don't give in to the transgender ideology phenomena, which didn't even exist until a few years ago. Let me say this again. Right now, in the United States of America, parents are having their children taken away from them for opposing a child's gender "transitioning."[9]

At a time when there is a national shortage of licensed foster care families, states like Vermont are revoking or refusing to renew licenses for families who are uncomfortable with new policies that require them to refer to a child by their chosen pronoun rather than by their biological sex. The new policies also require foster families to connect LGBTQ+ youth with "an LGBTQ adult role model to demonstrate options for the future" and to "bring young people to LGBTQ organizations and events in the community." Families who cannot in good conscience comply with these policies are being denied the opportunity to foster children in need.[10]

Gender transitioning can be big business and is being marketed to very young children and their parents. In August 2022, for instance, Boston Children's Hospital put out a series of videos that promoted what it called "gender-affirming hysterectomies" for young girls who identified as transgender. Videos in this series sought to answer such questions as "When Does a Child Know They're Transgender?"[11] The hospital's director of "gender multispecialty services" said that children will often know that they're transgender "from the moment they have any ability to express themselves." She says, "Parents will often tell us this. We have parents who tell us that with their kids, they knew from the minute they were born, practically. And actions like refusing to get a haircut or standing to urinate, refusing to stand to urinate, trying on siblings' clothing, playing with the 'opposite gender' toys, things like that."[12]

I saw the video. This is real. Can you imagine making a life-changing decision based on a child's actions before they can even speak? I was a tomboy growing up and wore nothing but boys surf shorts and T-shirts for years. I liked surfing and martial arts, and had no interest in Barbie dolls, dresses, or makeup. By Boston Children's Hospital standards, their expert advice to my parents would have been to get me on puberty blockers right away! Like most things in our childhood, the tomboy thing was a phase that I grew out of. While I still love surfing and martial arts, I also like wearing a dress every now and then.

According to a study from the *International Journal of Psychiatry*, more than 80 percent of kids who identify as transgender and seek medical intervention eventually lose their desire to identify as the opposite sex.[13] Countless so-called "transgender" youths have come to deeply regret their decisions, citing them as the worst mistakes of their lives.

In another video, another employee of Boston Children's Hospital claims that "a good portion of children do know as early as, seemingly, from the womb. They will express their gender identity as very young children. Some, as soon as they can talk, they might say phrases like 'I'm a boy,' or 'I'm going to be a woman,' or 'I'm going to be a mom.' Kids know very, very early."[14]

The doctors in this video note that in the Boston Children's Hospital gender clinic, they see children as young as two and three. "When they come into the clinic," a doctor says, "They'll talk to a psychologist.

We'll be talking to the family about how to best support that child, and how to make sure that child has the space and support to explore their gender and do well throughout their development."[15]

The doctor then goes on to explain that a "gender-affirming hysterectomy" is the same as a regular hysterectomy—a procedure typically done on older women and those who are at risk of certain diseases—in that it consists of the removal of the uterus, the cervix, and the fallopian tubes.

"Some gender-affirming hysterectomies," the doctor notes in a warm, inviting voice, "will also include the removal of the ovaries. But that's technically a separate procedure. . . . Not every gender-affirming hysterectomy includes that. And people who are getting gender-affirming hysterectomies do not have to have their ovaries removed."[16]

I know many adult women who for one reason or another have struggled with the decision to have a hysterectomy. For these so-called doctors to assume that a child who can barely speak somehow has the capacity to make this life-altering and irreversible decision is preposterous. These people who call themselves medical professionals are telling families who are often in distress that a five-year-old girl who likes playing with trucks, or a little boy who plays with his sister's Barbie and Ken dolls, is really crying out for medical intervention and possibly irreversible sex-change surgery—surgery that can never change their sex, which is written into their DNA, but will leave them permanently scarred physically, mentally, and emotionally. This is not only dangerous, it goes against the Hippocratic oath of "First, do no harm."

According to a research paper that was published in the *Journal of the American Medical Association*, there has been a 389 percent increase in children receiving mastectomies in recent years.[17] The UCLA School of Law's Williams Institute published a study noting that the number of kids identifying as transgender in the United States has doubled in just the past five years.[18]

The sudden spike in children who are confused about their gender identity, and therefore are being convinced that they must alter their body, is not an accident or a result of some natural phenomenon. It is the result of a concerted effort to transform our society into one where objective truth and reality no longer exist, where there are no boundaries, and where those in power dictate what is true and what is "accepted."

Unnecessary harmful chemicals and surgeries are being pushed on our kids, even though the long-term effects of these medical procedures are open to serious question, including the fact that the drugs commonly used to block the onset of puberty were recently tagged by the FDA as being linked to health problems including brain-swelling, loss of bone density, and other issues.[19]

The U.S. assistant secretary of health and human services, a man who identifies as a "transgender woman" named Rachel Levine, claimed that anyone who dissents or questions whether these treatments are a good idea must be driven by political motives.

"Trans youth," Levine said, "need to be supported. They need to be affirmed. They need to be empowered. There is no argument about the value and the importance of gender-affirming care. . . . There is *no argument*."[20] People like Levine can't win the argument based on facts, so they say there is no argument.

Of course, what the Biden-Harris administration means when they say "gender-affirming care" is much more dangerous than the nice, sanitized term makes it seem. For boys, it means a regimen of puberty blockers, some of which are used "off-label." After the pills, the boy might be transferred to surgeons, who will discuss plans for turning the boy's penis into a fake vagina. This is typically done by slicing into the skin of the penis, folding it back, and turning the nerves into a clitoris. These surgeries are irreversible and, studies have shown, cause a myriad of lifelong physical and emotional problems and trauma.

Of all the lies that the Biden-Harris administration has pushed on the American people, this one angers me more than most. This is not, as Rachel Levine might suggest, because I'm trying to push a particular political agenda, or because I'm trying to use transgender people as a "wedge issue."

It's because it's some of the most vulnerable people in our society—children—who are being harmed by some of the most powerful and influential people in our country, like the president of the United States, Democrats in Congress, the American Medical Association, and some of the biggest corporations in America like Target, Maybelline, and others. The propaganda media and Big Tech fulfill an essential task on behalf of the Democrat elite by amplifying their narrative and silencing any who dare to dissent, canceling accounts and censoring content that does not support their agenda, no matter how factual it is.

Regret

In the spring of 2023, I went to Nashville to speak at a Rally to End Child Mutilation, organized by Matt Walsh of the *Daily Wire*. A crowd of thousands gathered on the lawn of the state capitol, standing in solidarity to protect children. There were many speakers that day, but there was only one I really wanted to meet—a brave young teenager named Chloe Cole who was one of the many victims of this transgender ideology contagion. I stood off to the side as I watched Chloe walk to the podium with firm confident steps and deliver a short but impactful speech about her experiences. She has a small frame and is very petite. That day she had her hair in pigtail braids. She stood at the podium, took a deep breath, and began her speech. Her voice never wavered. She didn't hesitate. She was there on a mission, and every word cut through the noise.

When she was done, the crowd was cheering, and she started walking in my direction with a slight smile on her face. When she saw me, her eyes lit up. We gave each other a big hug, and I told her how incredible and inspiring she is to countless people here and around the world. She giggled a little, uncomfortable with the praise, and said that she had been wanting to meet me for a long time, too. I later had Chloe on my podcast, where we had a lengthy, heartfelt conversation about the heartbreaking and devastating journey that led her to this moment.

When Chloe Cole was young, she wasn't interested in hanging out with the other girls on her block. She didn't like wearing the newest clothes from Abercrombie & Fitch, playing with dolls, doing her makeup, or spending hours deciding what kind of dress to wear that day.

For the most part, Chloe preferred to stay inside by herself where she enjoyed making pencil sketches of fictional characters she invented. She experimented with oil paints and relaxed by playing video games like *Mass Effect*, *Call of Duty*, and *World of Warcraft*. This didn't make her popular with the girls at school, and Chloe began to develop serious anxiety.

Then, on Chloe's eleventh birthday, in a gift-wrapped box, Chloe got a new Apple iPhone, and she was elated. She would now be able to keep up with her peers thanks to their posts on Instagram. She'd have video games and YouTube videos available wherever she went, giving her something to do at school other than worry about who was making fun of her.

Slowly, as Chloe felt more and more isolated in her real life, she found a sense of community on social media, connecting with other people who dressed the way she did, talked the way she did, and seemed to be dealing with the same confusing problems that she was.

The more she looked, the more the algorithms fed her.

Soon, she was seeing more and more posts talking about things like "nonbinary," "gender nonconforming," and "trans"—all over the "For You" feed on Instagram. In these posts, they told her that if you were a girl who liked to wear your hair short and play video games, you were probably not a girl at all. You're probably a boy trapped in a girl's body, they said.

Chloe thought this was the answer she'd been looking for. At first, the changes Chloe made were small. She cut her hair even shorter and started to dress in clothes that she bought at the boy's section of Target. She lowered her voice slightly, and even bought a tight bandolier to keep her breasts, which had just started to show, from peeking through her clothes. But as Chloe continued to go through puberty, the new clothes weren't enough. On the advice of people she met online, she resolved to make a more serious change.

Remember, at this point, Chloe is twelve years old. While adults have the capacity and freedom to make their own decisions, consult with doctors, and begin whatever medication or body-altering surgeries they choose, the same cannot be said of children like Chloe whose brains aren't even close to being fully developed.

Chloe finally wrote her parents a note where she explained everything and left it on the kitchen table. She told them that she didn't feel right in her body, and that she knew beyond a shadow of a doubt that the reason was because she was really a boy who had been born in the wrong body. She said that she loved her parents, and that she would respect whatever they chose to do next, but she had decided to change her "gender."

Chloe was prepared for the worst. She had heard horror stories of parents freaking out. But Chloe's parents, much to her surprise, didn't react with anger. They were loving and supportive. They didn't know what to do next, but they wanted the best for their daughter.

At the age of twelve, they took Chloe to meet with therapists to discuss her desire to "transition." Looking back now, Chloe feels that a few more therapist sessions might have been all she needed. If she had been reassured that her feelings of anxiety, depression, and dissociation were common in adolescent girls, were almost always a passing stage, and that she didn't need to mutilate her body to feel better about herself, that may have been enough to prevent her from taking the next life-altering steps.

Instead of recommending more therapy, Chloe was quickly directed to see doctors who would provide her with puberty-blocking drugs and surgery. At no point was Chloe ever *seriously* informed of the risks associated with these procedures or told the truth about the physical damage they would inflict. The warnings she received came in hastily whispered asides. Shortly before she underwent surgery to remove her breasts, for instance, a doctor mentioned, in passing, that, after surgery, she would be unable to breastfeed a child. Right before she was prescribed drugs to block the onset of puberty, another doctor told her the drugs might make her permanently incapable of pregnancy.

Chloe didn't care. She was thirteen years old. She couldn't imagine what it was like to want to have children, so it wasn't a tough decision for her at the time.

When Chloe's parents expressed concern that the process was moving too fast—particularly when it came to things like hormone blockers and surgeries—they were told by a gender specialist that this was a matter of life and death.

"Either you can have a live son," he said to Chloe's parents, "or a dead daughter. The choice is yours."

Within just a few years, Chloe emerged from several operating rooms and gender clinics as a fourteen-year-old "boy," complete with a flat chest and a new gravelly way of speaking. Although she chose not to undergo the "bottom surgery" that would have given her a fake penis, Chloe announced to the world on Instagram that she was now Leo Cole, and her pronouns were he/him.

Praise came swiftly from her online community. Chloe, now Leo, was celebrated for bravely undergoing her "transition." Suddenly, it seemed, she had more online friends than ever. The more Chloe talked about how much her new identity was helping her mental health, the more likes and messages she got from her online supporters. She was a hero, they said, serving as a model of how good life could be once you took the leap into transitioning.

Real life, however, was a different story. In school, Chloe was having trouble getting along with her peers. Her grades were slipping. She began to feel even more uncomfortable in her body than she had before she started taking hormones. She began having deep regret and horrible thoughts about her inability ever to get pregnant or have a child.

To this day, she remembers almost bursting into tears in an introductory psychology class when she read about the bond between mothers and their children. The pain of realizing she might never experience that bond overwhelmed her.

Before long, Chloe began having suicidal thoughts—something she never experienced before she radically changed her body. As the frequency of the thoughts increased, she began to wonder if she had made a horrible mistake and reached out to some of her doctors.

Unsurprisingly, the doctors said her feelings were normal. When she told one of her surgeons that she was feeling extreme pain at the site of one surgery she had undergone, he told her to "put some Vaseline on it" and stop complaining; the pain, he insisted, would go away as long as she kept going forward with the transition.

When she later decided to de-transition, her doctors stopped returning her calls.

Unable to find help from her medical practitioners, Chloe started looking for answers online, and found that she wasn't alone. There was a community of people online who called themselves "de-transitioners" who had come to the realization that they had been lied to and were worse off now than before they started taking chemical castration pills and surgeries.

By the year 2022, shortly after Chloe stopped taking her hormones and began her de-transition process, the number of kids identifying as transgender in the United States had doubled from five years before.[21] Instead of wallowing in regret and the misery that her mistake brought her, she decided to turn her pain into something positive, speaking out against the so-called progressive politicians and activists who insist that so-called gender transition is the only way to "fix" kids who don't feel comfortable in their bodies.

The more Chloe speaks out, the more viciously she is attacked by the trans community. All the adoration and support they showed her previously vanished into thin air. They didn't care about her at all. This was never about her. It was about them and their influence. It was about the powerful Democrat elite in our society using and abusing children like Chloe as pawns in their greater objective of declaring themselves the ultimate authority and source of power—in their minds, even more powerful than God. They are the ones who can correct the "mistake" they claim God made; they are the ones who declare what is true and what is false; they declare who deserves freedom and who does not.

The Bottom Line

Family is the basic element of society and serves as the bedrock of civilization. We are stronger and more successful as a society when we have strong families.

We hear politicians talk a lot about being "pro-family" but so much of it is lip service used during election time to win a few votes. Even worse, the Democrat elite will label a policy "pro-family" even though it undermines the foundation of the family.

I have shared a few examples of this in this chapter, illustrating the extreme lengths the Democrat elite cabal is willing to go to get what they want—power. They are willing to destroy the most vulnerable among us and undermine parents and families as they designate themselves as the singular all-knowing authority who knows what's best for families and for our society as a whole.

There are more examples, of course, of the Democrat elite undermining families. Our deeply broken and dysfunctional social welfare system, for example, provides monetary incentives for single moms to never get married.

The Democrat elite celebrate abortion and encourage young pregnant women to abort their babies, as though it's nothing more serious than taking aspirin, rather than encourage women to visit pregnancy centers that can provide a safe place of support, knowledge, and a plethora of options available to them.

They claim to support families, yet adoption remains an intense and extremely expensive process that is limited to the wealthy and out of reach for most Americans, leaving children moving from one foster care home to another, and alone on the street when they turn eighteen.

They claim to support families, but through their defund the police programs and prosecutors favoring criminals over victims, it's clear they don't care about ensuring safe communities where parents can raise their children without worrying about whether they will come home at the end of the day.

Our country's elite see the well-being of people and families as an afterthought to the well-being of the economy. Their measure of success is whether or not someone has a college degree—the fancier, more expensive the school, the better. They often don't even care what the degree is in. They just assume that because you have a piece of paper with "Diploma" written across the top, you are a more intelligent, successful person. This has resulted in an entire generation of Americans buried in lifelong student loan debt,[22] unable to get a job in their chosen field, holding a piece of paper that has become increasingly meaningless. Thankfully, more businesses are recognizing that a piece of paper is not an accurate measure of a good hire. Nearly half of American businesses plan to remove bachelor's degrees as a prerequisite to hiring for certain positions, and 80 percent of employers said they are more likely to favor work experience over education when considering a new hire.[23]

Every month, the health of our country is measured by those in government and the media through unemployment numbers and gross domestic product. A good year means unemployment is down and GDP is up. But they are not measuring how many people in this country are actually happy. Many people who have good-paying jobs, fancy college degrees, and lots of money are unhappy and divorced, with children who won't talk to them. They're not measuring the deep sadness and longing of a new mother who wants nothing more than to raise her child at home; instead, the politicians say she should be grateful because they're giving her taxpayer dollars to hand over her child to a stranger at day care. They're not measuring the ever-increasing number of Americans on antidepressants because of the anxiety caused by their job or family life being in a shambles. On the other hand, the elite look down on a family with a median income of $50,000 a year, where one or both parents don't have a college degree, but spend quality time with their kids every day, are spiritually fulfilled, and happy with their life.

To the elite, we are all worker bees whose purpose in life is to fuel the machine of the nation's economy and the corporate industrial complex. The harder we work, the more taxes we pay, the more "revenue" the government is able to raise, which feeds into the establishment's ability to grow and build more power. They don't care about the people. They have forgotten that the purpose of government is to be limited, and defend our right to live free in the way that we choose.

The solution is simple: we need leaders—Democrats, Independents, and Republicans—to uphold the Constitution and put the well-being and interests of the people first. Our Founders placed the power in the hands of the American people to decide who we want to serve in our government—*our* government. When Election Day comes around, cast your vote carefully. Those who don't care about the people do not deserve the honor of serving the people in our government.

Epilogue

At Peace and Free or at War and Not Free—
the Choice Is Ours

On January 27, 1838, Abraham Lincoln delivered a speech to the Young Men's Lyceum of Springfield, Illinois. Lincoln saw this as an opportunity to underscore the vital importance of the rule of law—particularly as it relates to threats to U.S. institutions. What follows is an excerpt from that speech that deserves our serious contemplation.

> At what point then is the approach of danger to be expected? I answer, if it ever reach us, it must spring up amongst us. It cannot come from abroad. If destruction be our lot, we must ourselves be its author and finisher. As a nation of freemen, we must live through all time, or die by suicide. —Abraham Lincoln

It is difficult to witness what the Democrat elites are consciously orchestrating—be it the multifacted attack on the First Amendment, the defunding of police, undermining our Second Amendment right, politicizing our institutions to silence opposition, labeling and targeting half the population as "deplorables," "domestic terrorists," or "extremists," dividing us based on race, opening our borders to millions of illegal, unvetted migrants, allowing our cities to be overrun with crime, destroying our economy and driving our nation further into debt, rewarding media organizations that serve as propaganda tools of the elite, etc.—**without remembering Lincoln's warning: if this great nation dies, it will be by suicide.**

If we can agree that our country is headed rapidly in the wrong direction, the obvious next question is: *Now what?* Where do we go from here? What do we do?

Our future is in our hands.

It's easy to feel as if the vision our Founders had for our country has begun to fade. At times, we may feel like our voices aren't being heard or that we can't make a difference. I hear all the time from people who say to me, "Why bother voting? My vote won't make a difference," or "The system is rigged, why bother participating in it?"

Given the darkness, corruption, and abuse of power that hovers like a dark cloud above our country, it's understandable to feel overwhelmed, even hopeless.

But if we sit back and do nothing, we will lose the country we love, and those who hate our country and all that we stand for, win. And things will begin to move very quickly from the hardship and insanity that we see today, to catastrophic.

It is at this moment that we must look to the profound vision that our nation's Founders had for this country for inspiration.

We hold these truths to be self-evident, that all men are cre-
ated equal, that they are endowed by their Creator with cer-
tain unalienable Rights, that among these are Life, Liberty
and the pursuit of Happiness.—That to secure these rights,
Governments are instituted among Men, deriving their just
powers from the consent of the governed. —Declaration of
Independence

Our unalienable rights are endowed upon every one us by our Creator. Therefore, as long as God—whose very essence is love—exists, there is hope. Since God is eternal and will always exist, there will always be hope.

God's love is the light within each of our hearts, and His love is the answer to how we can heal our divides and come together around our common goal: defending the fundamental pillars of freedom that serve as the foundation of our country, and working toward a future of peace, freedom, security, and prosperity for all.

Love is the most powerful thing. It's what we in Hawaii call aloha—love, respect, and compassion for one another. It's not just a feeling. It's not weak or passive. It's a powerful force that motivates us to take action, to stand up for what's right, to fight for our freedom. Love for others, and for our country, is what motivates me to serve. It's what motivates my brothers and sisters in uniform to put our lives on the line to defend the security and freedom of the American people.

That love is what gives each and every one of us the courage to speak the truth, especially in the face of adversity, threats, and criticism.

It gives us the strength to fight for what's right and the humility to forgive those who've wronged us, overcome our differences, and move forward.

Love reminds us of who we really are as children of God and as Americans.

Although our flawed election system desperately needs to be fixed, our democratic process is still the best there is, and participating in this process is the only way we can fix what is broken. It works better than any other system ever created because it was created to keep the power in the hands of a free people, where an open marketplace of ideas thrives on discussion, differences, and debate.

But in order for this to work, it is essential that we remember that this government "of, by, and for the people" that our Founders envisioned for us demands—even requires—our involvement. A democratic republic can only be healthy and successful if we as citizens are informed and actively involved. To help save our great nation, we must participate—attend town meetings, get informed, and hold our elected leaders accountable. Speak out about the things that matter most to you, your family, and your friends. At a very minimum, vote. But don't blindly vote based on political party, name ID, or any other superficiality. Don't listen to the Democrat Party's mantra "Vote blue no matter who!" That blind team spirit mentality is exactly the thinking that got us into this mess. Vote for people who are truly public servants rather than self-serving career politicians. Vote for people who have demonstrated courage and commitment to upholding our Constitution and putting the well-being and interests of the American people and our country first, ahead of any personal or partisan interests.

If you are not satisfied with any of the candidates in your community, consider running for office yourself. If you don't want to run for public office, support candidates who align with your values by making a contribution, registering new voters, informing your friends and neighbors, and helping make sure they get out and vote.

> *That to secure these rights, Governments are instituted*
> *among Men, deriving their just powers from the consent*
> *of the governed.*

Those in power cannot remain there without the consent of the governed.

That's us. The power is in our hands.

The greatest challenge leaders in a democratic republic have is controlling the impulse to force their will on people, removing our freedom of choice because they think they know what's best for us and they need to protect us from making the "wrong" choice. No matter how much they claim to care about the people or democracy, leaders who think this way are acting like dictators.

I, like most Americans, would rather live in a society where I'm free to make the "wrong" decision and live with the consequences than have someone else make the "right" decision for me. This freedom to make our own decisions was the basis of the founding of our country. Elite politicians from both parties are terrified of our freedom and that we, the people, may actually begin to use our power. We, as a free people living in a free society, are the greatest threat to self-serving politicians and their power.

This is why they try so hard to control what information we see and what we are allowed to say. It's why they attack any political opposition that threatens their power. It's why the Democrat elite are doing all they possibly can to destroy their major opposition in 2024—former president Donald Trump—even going so far as declaring him unfit to be a candidate and barring him from being on the ballot. They are so terrified of our having the freedom to choose our next president—especially one who would have the courage to hold them accountable for their crimes—that they are willing to completely undermine our democracy and take away our right and freedom to vote for the candidate of our choosing.

We cannot allow these corrupt, self-serving politicians to remain in power. They care more about their political party, partisan ideology, and self-preservation than they do about the American people and our country. It's important to understand that they will stop at nothing in their reckless determination to hold on to power. If we fail to unite and vote them out of power, all that we love about our country will be lost.

Our freedom and our future are in our hands. Freedom is not free. We cannot lose sight of our potential and what we can accomplish when we, the people, stand together, and find common cause in the foundational principles upon which this country was built—a free people with the right to life, liberty, and pursuit of happiness. These are the ideals that drew me to serve this country in the first place, both in the military and in Congress.

Now is the time for us to spark a new political movement centered around making Rev. Martin Luther King Jr.'s dream a reality, inspired by aloha—love, respect, and hope.

We must protect the free speech of all Americans, speaking out against the censors on both sides who'd rather shut down ideas than engage in honest debate. When the free speech of one person is threatened—even when that speech is reprehensible to us—the free speech of all people is threatened.

The same goes for freedom of religion. In our America, the government must not be allowed to advocate for one religion over another, nor should it discriminate against and persecute those of one religion or another. The Pilgrims came from Europe escaping a state-sponsored religion so they could freely exercise their own beliefs. This right is enshrined in our Constitution. Freedom of religion does not mean freedom *from* religion. Real religion is love for God and is not attached to one religious sect or another. Real religion is a deeply personal relationship with God that exists within our own hearts. Government's role is to respect that relationship with God, our freedom to express and practice our religion and faith in the ways that we choose, or our freedom to not seek to develop our relationship with God at all.

Our Founders intentionally passed the Second Amendment right after the First. They knew how fragile this new, free democracy was, and how susceptible it would be to those who sought to abuse their power and take away our freedom. We must defend our right to bear arms, not only for recreational purposes, but to defend ourselves and our loved ones, and to serve as a check on the abuse of power by an increasingly tyrannical government.

We must stop the bipartisan warmongers of Washington who constantly beat their war drums, and have pushed us to the precipice of World War III and a nuclear catastrophe with the potential to destroy modern civilization many times over. As Albert Einstein said, "I know not with what weapons World War III will be fought, but World War IV will be fought with sticks and stones."

These are the people President Eisenhower warned us against in his farewell speech, who bend the knee to their bosses in the "military-industrial complex" and then shrug their shoulders and look the other way when the consequences of their actions prove costly, damaging, and potentially catastrophic for the rest of us.

We need leaders who are committed to peace, strength, and prosperity. We cannot be truly prosperous as a nation unless we are at peace. Unfortunately, war is sometimes necessary to defeat those foreign powers who threaten the safety, security, and freedom of the American people. As a soldier who has served over twenty-one years in our military, and still serves today, I know how critical it is that we stand ready to exact a decisive victory over those who seek to do us harm. But we must never forget that war must be a last resort, after all other avenues have been exhausted.

We need to elect leaders who are committed to upholding the rule of law, ensuring fair and just treatment under the law and safe communities and streets. Our leaders must take immediate action to secure our borders, understanding that without secure borders we have no nation.

We need leaders who appreciate the importance of families, and respect that parents know what is best for their children. Parents must have the freedom to choose what kind of education is best for their children and raise them according to their value system—not one imposed upon them by big government.

We need to elect leaders who understand that in order for us to remain prosperous as a people and as a nation for generations to come, we must be custodians of the blessings Mother Earth provides, protecting clean water, clean air, and the stunning mountain ranges, open plains, rivers, and oceans we treasure and enjoy.

We need to elect righteous leaders who are compassionate and care about the well-being of others and our society; leaders who are committed to the Constitution and strike the delicate and necessary balance between protecting our individual freedom and making decisions based on what's in the best interests of our country.

In our America, we will come together inspired by love—love for God, for others, and for our country. We will heed Rev. Martin Luther King's call, judging one another based on the content of our character rather than the color of our skin, and treating each other with respect—aloha—recognizing one another as fellow Americans and children of God, no matter our background, race, creed, or religion.

There is so much potential and possibility for our America if we choose to step up and take action.

Join me in choosing to end the downward spiral into darkness that the Democrat elite have imposed on us and our nation. Join me in leading a movement toward a future where Americans are more united, free, peaceful, and prosperous than ever before. To bring about that bright future, we must heed the call to action rendered to us in the Declaration of Independence and stand together to save our country and defend our republic.

One of the most common laments of people who lose a loved one to suicide is, "If only we'd known . . . we had no warning." One would need to be blind not to see that those in power in America today are leading this great nation toward the "suicide" Abraham Lincoln feared. We won't be able to say we had no warning.

Let us come together not as partisan adversaries but as Americans bound by our shared love of our country to ensure its survival.

Notes

Prologue

1 "Republican Official Threatens to Kick Biden off Ballot as Trump Payback," NBCNews.com, January 6, 2024, https://www.nbcnews.com/politics/2024-election/missouri-republican-secretary-of-state-biden-trump-ballot-rcna132600.

Chapter 1

1 Robert K. Hur, Report from special counsel Robert K. Hur February 2024, February 5, 2024, https://www.justice.gov/storage/report-from-special-counsel-robert-k-hur-february-2024.pdf.

2 Franklin Foer, "Was a Trump Server Communicating with Russia?" *Slate*, October 31, 2016, https://www.slate.com/articles/news_and_politics/cover_story/2016/10/was_a_server_registered_to_the_trump_organization_communicating_with_russia.html.

3 "Hillary Clinton Did It," *Wall Street Journal*, May 20, 2022, https://www.wsj.com/articles/hillary-clinton-did-it-robby-mook-michael-sussmann-donald-trump-russia-collusion-alfa-bank-11653084709.

4 Dan Merica, "Hillary Clinton Suggests Russians Are 'grooming' Tulsi Gabbard for Third-Party Run," CNN, October 21, 2019, https://www.cnn.com/2019/10/18/politics/hillary-clinton-tulsi-gabbard/index.html.

5 "Trump Indicted in New York," *New York Times*, March 30, 2023, https://www.nytimes.com/live/2023/03/30/nyregion/trump-indictment-news.

6 Chelsia Rose Marcius and Ed Shanahan, "Major Crimes Rose 22 Percent in New York City, Even as Shootings Fell," *New York Times*, January 5, 2023, https://www.nytimes.com/2023/01/05/nyregion/new-york-crime-stats.html.

7 "Remarks by President Biden on the Continued Battle for the Soul of the Nation," The White House, September 1, 2022, https://www.whitehouse.gov/briefing-room/speeches-remarks/2022/09/01/remarks-by-president-bidenon-the-continued-battle-for-the-soul-of-the-nation/.

8　　Mayhill Fowler, "Obama: No Surprise That Hard-Pressed Pennsylvanians Turn Bitter," *HuffPost*, November 17, 2008, https://www.huffpost.com /entry/obama-no-surprise-that-ha_b_96188.

9　　Kamal Sultan for Dailymail.Com, "Outrage as Biden Administration Admits Surveilling Americans' Private Financial Transactions for Words like 'Maga' 'trump' and 'Kamala' in Wake of Jan. 6 Riots . . . with People Buying Bibles on Top of Their Watchlist," Daily Mail Online, February 9, 2024, https://www.dailymail.co.uk/news/article-13067751 /Outrage-Biden-administration-admits-surveilling-Americans-private -financial-transactions-words-like-MAGA-Trump-Kamala-wake-Jan-6 -riots-people-buying-BIBLES-watchlist.html.

10　　Nancy Pelosi (@SpeakerPelosi), "The Grand Jury has acted upon the facts and the law. . . . ," Twitter, March 30, 2023, 8:15 p.m., https://twitter .com/SpeakerPelosi/status/1641594971462541315.

11　　"NYC Giving Pre-Paid Debit Cards to Asylum Seeker Families for Food, Baby Supplies," CBS News, February 8, 2024, https://www.cbsnews .com/newyork/news/nyc-giving-pre-paid-debit-cards-to-asylum-seeker -families-for-food-baby-supplies/.

12　　Melissa Koenig, "Army VET, 94, Kicked out of NYC Nursing Home to Make Room for Migrants," *New York Post*, November 30, 2023, https: //nypost.com/2023/11/30/news/army-vet-kicked-out-of-nyc-nursing -home-to-make-room-for-migrants/.

13　　Joseph MacKinnon, "'The Big Scam Nobody Is Talking about': House Democrat Makes Damning Admission on Why She Needs Illegal Aliens," Conservative Review, January 10, 2024, https://www.conservativereview .com/the-big-scam-nobody-is-talking-about-house-democrat-makes -damning-admission-on-why-she-needs-illegal-aliens-2666919422.html.

14　　Jim Mendoza, "Council Passes Abandoned Property Bill," *Hawaii News Now*, December 8, 2011, https://www.hawaiinewsnow.com /story/16214212/council-passes-abandoned-property-bill/.

15　　Mariame Kaba, "Yes, We Mean Literally Abolish the Police," *New York Times*, June 12, 2020, https://www.nytimes.com/2020/06/12/opinion /sunday/floyd-abolish-defund-police.html.

16　　Hans A. von Spakovsky and Charles Stimson, "FBI, Justice Department Twist Federal Law to Arrest, Charge Pro-Life Activist," Heritage Foundation, September 28, 2022, https://www.heritage.org/crime

-and-justice/commentary/fbi-justice-department-twist-federal-law-arrest
-charge-pro-life.

17 "Justice Department Addresses Violent Threats against School Officials
and Teachers," Department of Justice, Office of Public Affairs, October
4, 2021, https://www.justice.gov/opa/pr/justice-department-addresses
-violent-threats-against-school-officials-and-teachers.

Chapter 2

1   Franklin D. Roosevelt, "Address to the Congress Asking That a State of
War Be Declared between the United States and Japan," December 8, 1941,
https://www.loc.gov/resource/afc1986022.afc1986022_ms2201/?st=text.

2   "Executive Order 9066: Resulting in Japanese-American
Incarceration (1942)," National Archives, https://www.archives.gov
/milestone-documents/executive-order-9066

3   June Watanabe, "Lyrics Here to Combat Team's 'Go for Broke,'"
Honolulu Star-Bulletin, April 22, 2000, https://archives.starbulletin
.com/2000/04/22/news/kokualine.html.

4   Joanne Lee, "The Most Decorated Unit in American History,"
Dartmouth.edu, accessed February 14, 2024, https://www.dartmouth.
edu/~hist32/History/S28%20-%20442nd.htm#:~:text=For%20their%20
valor%20the%20442nd,one%20Congressional%20Medal%20of%20
Honor.

5   "Japanese-American Incarceration During World War II," National
Archives, https://www.archives.gov/education/lessons/japanese
-relocation.

6   Richard Blumenthal, "FISA Secrecy Must End," *Politico*, July 14, 2013,
https://www.politico.com/story/2013/07/fisa-court-process-must
-be-unveiled-094127.

7   Glenn Greenwald, "NSA Collecting Phone Records of Millions of Verizon
Customers Daily," *The Guardian*, June 6, 2013, https://www.theguardian
.com/world/2013/jun/06/nsa-phone-records-verizon-court-order.

8   Bill Chappell, "Clapper Apologizes for Answer on NSA's Data
Collection," NPR, July 2, 2013, https://www.npr.org/sections/the
two-way/2013/07/02/198118060/clapper-apologizes-for-answer-on-nsas
-data-collection.

9   "Senate Select Committee to Study Governmental Operations with
Respect to Intelligence Activities," United States Senate, https://www

.senate.gov/about/powers-procedures/investigations/church-committee
.htm.

10   Mallory Shelbourne, "Schumer: Trump 'Really Dumb' for Attacking
Intelligence Agencies," The Hill, January 3, 2017, https://thehill.com
/homenews/administration/312605-schumer-trump-being-really-dumb
-by-going-after-intelligence-community/.

11   "The Pentagon Papers: Secrets, Lies and Audiotape," National Security
Archive, George Washington University, https://nsarchive2.gwu.edu
/NSAEBB/NSAEBB48/nixon.html.

12   Bill Trott, "Daniel Ellsberg, Who Leaked 'Pentagon Papers,' Dies
at 92," Reuters, June 17, 2023, https://www.reuters.com/world/us
/pentagon-papers-whistleblower-daniel-ellsberg-dead-after-terminal
-cancer-2023–06-16/.

13   Charlie Savage, "Why the Pentagon Papers Leaker Tried to Get
Prosecuted Near His Life's End," New York Times, June 18, 2023, https:
//www.nytimes.com/2023/06/18/us/politics/daniel-ellsberg-espionage
-act-pentagon-papers.html.

14   "Another Chilling Leak Investigation" (opinion) New York Times,
May 21, 2013, https://www.nytimes.com/2013/05/22/opinion/another
-chilling-leak-investigation.html.

15   Erick Tucker and Alanna Durkin Richer, "How Much Prison
Time Could Trump Face? Past Cases Brought Steep Punishment
for Document Hoarders," Associated Press, June 15, 2023, https:
//apnews.com/article/donald-trump-classified-documents-espionage-act
-dc9d5d46f61809fb5aa1d972f47bed6a.

16   Matthew Loh, "Canada Says It Will Freeze the Bank Accounts of 'Freedom
Convoy' Truckers Who Continue Their Anti-Vaccine Mandate Blockades,"
Business Insider, February 14, 2022, https://www.businessinsider.com
/trudeau-canada-freeze-bank-accounts-freedom-convoy-truckers
-2022–2.

17   Senator Elizabeth Warren, "Senator Warren and Representative Dean
Urge Bank CEOs to Adopt New Code for Gun and Ammunition
Retailers," September 2, 2022, https://www.warren.senate.gov/oversight
/letters/senator-warren-and-representative-dean-urge-bank-ceos-to
-adopt-new-code-for-gun-and-ammunition-retailers.

18   Carlos Perona Calvete, "'This Is Not a Big Brother Project': Digital
Currency and Political Control," European Conservative, July 6, 2023,

https://europeanconservative.com/articles/analysis/this-is-not-a
-big-brother-project-digital-currency-and-political-control/.

19 Benjamin Franklin, "Pennsylvania Assembly: Reply to the Governor, 11
November 1755," Founders Online, National Archives, https://founders
.archives.gov/documents/Franklin/01–06-02–0107.

Chapter 3

1 Ian Schwartz, "Del. Stacey Plaskett to RFK Jr.: 'This Is Not The
Kind Of Free Speech That I Know Of,' Free Speech Is Not Absolute,"
RealClearPolitics, July 20, 2023, https://www.realclearpolitics.com
/video/2023/07/20/del_stacey_plaskett_to_rfk_jr_this_is_not_the_kind
_of_free_speech_that_i_know_of_free_speech_is_not_absolute.html.

2 Scott Stump, "Prince Harry Draws Criticism for Calling First Amendment
'Bonkers,'" *Today*, May 18, 2021, https://www.today.com/news/prince
-harry-draws-criticism-calling-first-amendment-bonkers-t218740.

3 Jon Brown, "UK Government Admits 'Inappropriate' to Argue Bible
'Offensive' in Case against Christian Street Preacher," Fox News,
December 19, 2022, https://www.foxnews.com/world/uk-government
-admits-inappropriate-argue-bible-offensive-case-christian-street
-preacher.

4 Caleb Howe, "'No to The Soviet Politburo!': Wasserman Schultz Leads
Dem Effort to Stop RFK Jr. 'Degradation' in Chaotic House Hearing
Vote," *Mediaite*, July 20, 2023, https://www.mediaite.com/politics
/no-to-the-soviet-politburo-wasserman-schultz-leads-dem-effort-to-stop
-rfk-jr-degradation-in-chaotic-house-hearing-vote/.

5 Julia Mueller, "Democrats Tear into RFK Jr. during Weaponization
Hearing," *The Hill*, July 20, 2023, https://thehill.com/homenews/house
/4107697-democrats-tear-into-rfk-jr-during-weaponization-hearing.

6 Josh Christenson, "Robert F. Kennedy Jr. Slams Democrats for Bid
'to Censor a Censorship Hearing,'" *New York Post*, July 20, 2023,
https://nypost.com/2023/07/20/rfk-jr-slams-dems-for-trying-to-censor
-a-censorship-hearing/.

7 Mary Margaret Olohan, "Berkeley Professor Urges Followers to
Steal, Burn Book on Trans 'Craze Seducing Our Daughters,'" The
Daily Caller, November 15, 2020, https://dailycaller.com/2020/11/15
/berkeley-professor-burn-book-trans-abigail-shrier/.

8   Charlotte Hays, "Some in ACLU Have New Cause: Book Banning," Independent Women's Forum, November 16, 2020, https://www.iwf .org/2020/11/16/some-in-aclu-have-new-cause-book-banning/.

9   Jeffrey A. Trachtenberg, "Penguin Random House Stands by Plan to Publish Amy Coney Barrett's Book," *Wall Street Journal*, October 31, 2022, https://www.wsj.com/articles/penguin-random-house-stands-by -plan-to-publish-amy-coney-barretts-book-11667248264.

10   Jonathan Turley, "Pew: Seventy Percent of Democrats and Democratic-Leaning Independents Support Speech Limits," Jonathan Turley, July 27, 2023, https://jonathanturley.org/2023/07/27/pew-seventy-percent-of -democrats-and-democratic-leaning-independents-support-speech -limits/.

11   Michael Powell, "Once a Bastion of Free Speech, the A.C.L.U. Faces an Identity Crisis," *The New York Times*, June 6, 2021, https://www .nytimes.com/2021/06/06/us/aclu-free-speech.html.

12   Lachlan Markay, "Gmail Filters More Likely to Weed Out GOP Emails," *Axios*, April 10, 2022, https://www.axios.com/2022/04/10 /gmail-filters-more-likely-to-weed-out-gop-emails.

13   Peter Kasperowicz, "206 Democrats Vote against Bill Banning Federal Officials from Policing Online Speech," Fox News, March 9, 2023, https://www.foxnews.com/politics/democrats-vote-against-bill-banning -federal-officials-policing-online-speech.

14   Ibid.

15   Miranda Devine, "Ex-CIA Chief Spills on How He Got Spies to Write False Hunter Biden Laptop Letter to 'Help Biden,'" *New York Post*, April 20, 2023, https://nypost.com/2023/04/20 /biden-campaign-pushed-spies-to-write-false-hunter-laptop-letter/.

16   Steven Nelson, "FBI 'Verified' Authenticity of Hunter Biden's Abandoned Laptop in November 2019: IRS Whistleblower," *New York Post*, June 22, 2023, https://nypost.com/2023/06/22/fbi-verified-authenticity-of -hunter-bidens-abandoned-laptop-in-november-2019-irs-whistleblower -gary-shapley/.

17   Natasha Bertrand, "Hunter Biden story is Russian disinfo, dozens of former intel officials say," *Politico*, October 19, 2020, https://www.politico.com /news/2020/10/19/hunter-biden-story-russian-disinfo-430276.

18   Jessica Chasmar, "Biden Claims That Hunter Laptop Was 'Russian Disinformation' Debunked by His Own Son," Fox News, February 2,

2023, https://www.foxnews.com/politics/biden-claims-hunter-laptop-russian-disinformation-debunked-his-own-son.

19 "New Testimony Reveals Secretary Blinken and Biden Campaign behind the Infamous Public Statement on the Hunter Biden Laptop," House Judiciary Committee, April 20, 2023, https://judiciary.house.gov/media/press-releases/new-testimony-reveals-secretary-blinken-and-biden-campaign-behind-infamous.

20 Kanishka Singh, "US Judge Restricts Biden Officials from Contact with Social Media Firms," Reuters, July 5, 2023, https://www.reuters.com/legal/judge-blocks-us-officials-communicating-with-social-media-companies-newspaper-2023–07-04/.

21 Thomas Jefferson to Philip Mazzei, 24 April 1796, Founders Online, National Archives, https://founders.archives.gov/documents/Jefferson/01–29-02–0054-0002.

22 "Special Message to the Congress: The President's First Economic Report," January 8, 1947, The American Presidency Project, UC Santa Barbara, https://www.presidency.ucsb.edu/documents/special-message-the-congress-the-presidents-first-economic-report.

Chapter 4

1 Ben Smith, "Obama on Small-town Pa.: Clinging to Religion, Guns, Xenophobia," *Politico*, April 11, 2008, https://www.politico.com/blogs/ben-smith/2008/04/obama-on-small-town-pa-clinging-to-religion-guns-xenophobia-007737.

2 "American Originals," National Archives, https://www.archives.gov/exhibits/american_originals/inaugtxt.html

3 Amy Sullivan, "The Party Faithful—Jesus Bumps and God Gaps," *New York Times*, February 10, 2008, https://www.nytimes.com/2008/02/10/books/chapters/1st-chapter-party-faithful.html.

4 "Fact Check: The 2020 DNC Did Not Omit 'under God' from Every Pledge of Allegiance," Reuters, August 26, 2020, https://www.reuters.com/article/uk-factcheck-pledge-allegiance-dnc/fact-check-the-2020-dnc-did-not-omit-under-god-from-every-pledge-of-allegiance-idUSKBN25M1OO.

5 Jon Brown, "Anti-Christian Hostility Reaching 'Unprecedented' Levels in Culture, Government under Biden, Observers Warn," Fox News, April 13, 2023, https://www.foxnews.com/us/anti-christian-hostility-reaching-unprecedented-levels-culture-government-under-biden-observers-warn.

6   "Little Sisters of the Poor v. Azar," The Becket Fund for Religious Liberty, https://www.becketlaw.org/case/littlesisters/.

7   Alexander Hall, "Purported FBI Document Suggests Agency May be Targeting Catholics Who Attend Latin Mass," Fox News, February 9, 2023, https://www.foxnews.com/media/purported-fbi-document -suggests-agency-targeting-catholics-attend-latin-mass.

8   Katherine Knott, "Biden Administration to Rescind Part of Religious Freedom Rule," *Inside Higher Ed*, February 22, 2023, https://www .insidehighered.com/news/2023/02/23/biden-administration-rescind -part-.trumps-free-inquiry-rule.

9   Alexandra DeSanctis, "A Brief History of Kamala Harris and the Knights of Columbus," Yahoo, October 9, 2020, https://www.yahoo.com/now /brief-history-kamala-harris-knights-140302014.html.

10 Valerie Richardson, "Kamala Harris, Mazie Hirono Target Brian Buescher Knights of Columbus Membership," *Washington Times*, December 30, 2018, https://www.washingtontimes.com/news/2018 /dec/30/kamala-harris-mazie-hirono-target-brian-buescher-k/.

11 James Crump, "'The Dogma Lives Loudly in You': Dianne Feinstein's Grilling of Trump SCOTUS Frontrunner for Her Devout Catholicism Goes Viral," The Independent, September 22, 2020, https://www .independent.co.uk/news/world/americas/us-politics/amy-coney-barrett -supreme-court-diana-feinstein-ruth-bader-ginsburg-b512741.html.

12 "Transcript: JFK's Speech on His Religion," NPR, September 12, 1960, https://www.npr.org/templates/story/story.php?storyId=16920600.

13 Tulsi Gabbard, "Elected Leaders Who Weaponize Religion Are Playing a Dangerous Game," *The Hill*, January 8, 2019, https://thehill.com/blogs /congress-blog/religious-rights/424362-elected-leaders-who-weaponize -religion-are-playing-a/

14 John D. Sutter, "Hawaii's Homeless Candidate for Congress," CNN, October 29, 2012, https://www.cnn.com/2012/10/29/opinion/ctl-kawika -crowley-homeless-candidate-hawaii/index.html.

15 Kyveli Diener, "Tulsi Gabbard Is the Surfing Congresswoman Who Could Actually Save Our Environment," *The Intertia*, August 16, 2018, https: //www.theinertia.com/surf/tulsi-gabbard-is-the-surfing-congresswoman -who-could-actually-save-our-environment/.

16 "Charleston Victim's Mother Tells Dylann Roof 'I Forgive You' as He's Sentenced to Death," ABC News, January 11, 2017, https://abcnews

.go.com/US/charleston-victims-mother-tells-dylann-roof-forgive/story
?id=44704096.

17 Martin Luther King Jr., "Loving Your Enemies," *Strength in Love* (Harper & Rowe, 1963), qtd. in Cynthia L. Haven, "Martin Luther King Jr. Quote Goes Viral. Fake? Not Really . . .," *The Book Haven*, https://bookhaven.stanford.edu/2011/05/martin-luther-king-jr -quote-goes-viral-is-it-a-fake-not-really/.

18 Noel Paul Stookey, "Wedding Song (There Is Love)," Public Domain Foundation, 1971, https://noelpaulstookey.com/music/lyrics/wedding -song-there-is-love/.

Chapter 5

1 Gregory Krieg and Joshua Berlinger, "Hillary Clinton: Donald Trump would be Putin's 'puppet,'" CNN, October 20, 2016, https://www.cnn .com/2016/10/19/politics/clinton-puppet-vladimir-putin-trump/index .html.

2 Ja'han Jones, "Trump (Still) Behaving like a Pro-Russia Agent," MSNBC, January 30, 2023, https://www.msnbc.com/the-reidout/reidout-blog /trump-russia-putin-ukraine-rcna68247

3 Kate Sullivan and Laura Jarrett, "McCabe: 'I think it's possible' Trump is a Russian asset," CNN, February 20, 2019, https://www.cnn .com/2019/02/19/politics/andrew-mccabe-trump-law-enforcement/index .html.

4 Craig Unger, "Donald Trump Was Everything Vladimir Putin Could Have Wished For," *New Republic*, March 2, 2022, https: //newrepublic.com/article/165553/donald-trump-everything -vladimir-putin-wished-russian-asset.

5 Tulsi Gabbard, (@TulsiGabbard), "HAWAII - THIS IS A FALSE ALARM. . . .," Twitter, January 13, 2018, 1:19 p.m., https://twitter .com/TulsiGabbard/status/952243723525677056.

6 "A Time of Unprecedented Danger: It Is 90 Seconds to Midnight," *Bulletin of the Atomic Scientists*, January 24, 2023, https://thebulletin .org/doomsday-clock/current-time/.

7 "The Reagan-Gorbachev Statement: Background to #ReaffirmOur Future," European Leadership Network, November 19, 2021, https: //www.europeanleadershipnetwork.org/commentary/the-reagan -gorbachev-statement-background-to-reaffirmourfuture/.

8   "The Cuban Missile Crisis, October 1962," U.S. Department of State, accessed February 16, 2024, https://history.state.gov /milestones/1961–1968/cuban-missile-crisis#:~:text=After%20the%20 failed%20U.S.%20attempt,missiles%20in%20Cuba%20to%20deter.

9   "The Great Seal," National Museum of American Diplomacy, March 19, 2018, https://diplomacy.state.gov/the-great-seal/.

10   John F. Kennedy, "Commencement Address at American University, Washington, D.C., June 10, 1963," John F. Kennedy Presidential Library and Museum, https://www.jfklibrary.org/archives/other-resources /john-f-kennedy-speeches/american-university-19630610.

11   Mark Hertling and Molly K. McKew, "Putin's Attack on the U.S. Is Our Pearl Harbor," *Politico*, July 16, 2018, https://www.politico.com/magazine /story/2018/07/16/putin-russia-trump-2016-pearl-harbor-219015/.

12   Steve Holland, "Trump Says He Thinks He Could Have a Good Relationship with Putin," Reuters, April 3, 2018, https://www.reuters .com/article/us-usa-trump-russia-putin/trump-says-he-thinks-he-could -have-a-good-relationship-with-putin-idUSKCN1HA2D8/.

13   "President Dwight D. Eisenhower's Farewell Address (1961)," National Archives, https://www.archives.gov/milestone-documents/president -dwight-d-eisenhowers-farewell-address#:~:text=In%20the%20 councils%20of%20government,power%20exists%20and%20will%20 persist.

14   Mary Ellen Cagnassola, "Defense Contractors Benefited from Nearly Half of $14 Trillion Spent for Afghan War: Study," *Newsweek*, September 13, 2021, https://www.newsweek.com/defense-contractors -benefited-nearly-half-14-trillion-spent-afghan-war-study-1628485.

15   Kennedy, "Commencement Address."

16   Nandita Bose, "Biden Cites Cuban Missile Crisis in Describing Putin's Nuclear Threat," Reuters, October 6, 2022, https://www.reuters .com/world/biden-cites-cuban-missile-crisis-describing-putins-nuclear -threat-2022-10-07/.

17   Márton Losonczi, "Russia-Ukraine Peace Was Blocked by Western Powers, Former Israeli Prime Minister Claims," *Hungarian Conservative*, February 7, 2023, https://www.hungarianconservative.com/articles /current/russia_ukraine-peace_blocked_western_powers_naftali _bennett_mediationraeli-prime-minister-claims/.

18 Kevin Liptak and Maegan Vazquez, "Biden Says Putin 'Cannot Remain in Power,'" CNN, March 26, 2022, https://www.cnn.com/2022/03/26/politics/biden-warsaw-saturday/index.html.

19 Missy Ryan and Annabelle Timsit, "U.S. Wants Russian Military 'Weakened' from Ukraine Invasion, Austin Says," *Washington Post*, April 25, 2022, https://www.washingtonpost.com/world/2022/04/25/russia-weakened-lloyd-austin-ukraine-visit/.

20 "U.S. Security Assistance to Ukraine," Congressional Research Service, January 3, 2024, https://crsreports.congress.gov/product/pdf/IF/IF12040.

21 Catie Edmondson and Emily Cochrane, "Senate Overwhelmingly Approves $40 Billion in Aid to Ukraine, Sending It to Biden," *New York Times*, May 19, 2022, https://www.nytimes.com/2022/05/19/us/politics/senate-passes-ukraine-aid.html.

22 Letter from Members of the Congressional Progressive Caucus to the President, October 24, 2022, https://progressives.house.gov/_cache/files/5/5/5523c5cc-4028-4c46-8ee1-b56c7101c764/B7B3674EFB12D933EA4A2B97C7405DD4.10-24-22-cpc-letter-for-diplomacy-on-russia-ukraine-conflict.pdf.

23 Andrew Solender, "House Progressive Withdraws Ukraine Letter after Backlash," *Axios*, October 25, 2022, https://www.axios.com/2022/10/25/house-progressives-letter-ukraine-pramila-jayapal.

24 William J. Perry, "How the U.S. Lost Russia—and How We Can Restore Relations," *Outrider*, September 5, 2022, https://outrider.org/nuclear-weapons/articles/how-us-lost-russia-and-how-we-can-restore-relations.

25 Ibid.

26 George F. Kennan, "A Fateful Error," *New York Times*, February 5, 1997, https://www.nytimes.com/1997/02/05/opinion/a-fateful-error.html.

27 Ibid.

28 "Iraq Conflict Has Killed a Million Iraqis: Survey," Reuters, January 30, 2008, https://www.reuters.com/article/us-iraq-deaths-survey/iraq-conflict-has-killed-a-million-iraqis-survey-idUSL3048857920080130.

29 Ahmed Twaij, "Let's Remember Madeleine Albright for Who She Really Was," Al Jazeera, March 25, 2022, https://www.aljazeera.com/opinions/2022/3/25/lets-remember-madeleine-albright-as-who-she-really-was#:~:text=%E2%80%9CWe%20have%20heard%20that%20half,the%20price%20is%20worth%20it.%E2%80%9D.

30 "Remarks by President Biden on Security Assistance to Ukraine," White House, May 3, 2022, https://www.whitehouse.gov/briefing-room /speeches-remarks/2022/05/03/remarks-by-president-biden-on-the -security-assistance-to-ukraine/; Jake Werner, "What Biden Means When He Says We're Fighting 'Global Battle for Democracy,'" *Responsible Statecraft*, April 1, 2023, https://responsiblestatecraft.org/2023/03/31 /what-biden-means-when-he-says-were-fighting-global-battle-for -democracy/.

31 Dewi Fortuna Anwar, "A Rules-Based Order in the Indo-Pacific: A View from Jakarta," U.S. Department of Defense, https://media.defense. gov/2020/Dec/06/2002546899/-1/-1/1/ANWAR.PDF.

32 Mike Lillis, "Clyburn Slams Trump, Others Praising Putin; 'Domestic Enemies," *The Hill*, February 27, 2022, https://thehill.com/homenews /house/595936-clyburn-slams-trump-others-praising-putin-domestic -enemies/.

33 "Judiciary Republicans to Garland: Are Concerned Parents Domestic Terrorists or Not?" (press release), Chuck Grassley, December 6, 2021, https://www.grassley.senate.gov/news/news-releases/judiciary -republicans-to-garland-are-concerned-parents-domestic-terrorists-or -not.

Chapter 6

1   David Remnick, *The Bridge: The Life and Rise of Barack Obama* (New York: Vintage Books, 2010), 6.

2   Vanessa Robinson, "Blood at the Ballot Box: The Murders of Jimmie Lee Jackson, the Rev. James Reeb, and Viola Liuzzo," *Medium*, October 30, 2020, https://vrob125.medium.com/blood-at-the-ballot-box-the -murders-of-jimmie-lee-jackson-the-rev-james-reeb-and-viola-liuzzo -61ba9025ddb3.

3   "Wallace Orders Troopers to Stop Negro Marchers," UPI, March 6, 1965, https://www.upi.com/Archives/1965/03/06/Wallace-orders -troopers-to-stop-Negro-marchers/2541162885347/.

4   John Lewis, *Walking with the Wind: A Memoir of the Movement* (Simon & Schuster, 1998), 326.

5   Christopher Klein, "How Selma's 'Bloody Sunday' Became a Turning Point in the Civil Rights Movement," History, March 6, 2015, https://www .history.com/news/selma-bloody-sunday-attack-civil-rights-movement.

6 Ibid.

7 Lewis, *Walking with the Wind*, 327.

8 Ibid.

9 "Dr. Martin Luther King Jr., 'How Long? Not Long?' (25 March 1965)," Voices of Democracy, https://voicesofdemocracy.umd.edu/dr-martin-luther-king-jr-long-not-long-speech-text/.

10 "Read Martin Luther King Jr.'s 'I Have a Dream' Speech in Its Entirety," NPR, speech delivered August 28, 1963, https://www.npr.org/2010/01/18/122701268/i-have-a-dream-speech-in-its-entirety.

11 Michael Stramber, "A Universal Perspective Is Key to Diversity and Equity in Schools," *The Hill*, October 12, 2021, https://thehill.com/changing-america/opinion/576345-prioritizing-our-universal-ties-instead-of-identity-is-the-key-to/.

12 Rich Lowry, "The Toxic World-View of Ta-Nehisi Coates," Politico, July 22, 2015, https://www.politico.com/magazine/story/2015/07/the-toxic-world-view-of-ta-nehisi-coates-120512/.

13 Robin DiAngelo, *White Fragility: Why It's So Hard for White People to Talk about Racism* (Boston: Beacon Press, 2018), 91.

14 Ibid., 149.

15 Ibid., 150.

16 Douglas Murray, *The War on the West* (New York: Broadside Books, 2022).

17 "Ibram X. Kendi defines what it means to be an antiracist," Penguin Random House UK, June 9, 2020, https://www.penguin.co.uk/articles/2020/06/ibram-x-kendi-definition-of-antiracist.

18 Martin Luther King Jr., "Address to the House of Representatives of the First Legislature, State of Hawaii, on 17 September 1959," Martin Luther King Jr. Institute, Stanford University, https://kinginstitute.stanford.edu/king-papers/documents/address-house-representatives-first-legislature-state-hawaii-17-september-1959.

Chapter 7

1 Maud Maron, "It's Time to Get Serious about Saving Girl's and Women's Sports," *Newsweek*, March 18, 2022, https://www.newsweek.com/its-time-get-serious-about-saving-girls-womens-sports-opinion-1689217.

2   Dan Avery, "Trans Women Retain Athletic Edge after a Year of Hormone Therapy, Study Finds," *NBC News*, January 5, 2021, https://www.nbcnews.com/feature/nbc-out/trans-women-retain-athletic-edge-after-year-hormone-therapy-study-n1252764.

3   "Rip Curl Women's Campaign: Controversy over Inclusion of Trans . . .," News.com.au, January 30, 2024, https://www.news.com.au/sport/sports-life/rip-curl-latest-subject-of-a-fervent-go-woke-go-broke-campaign/news-story/d4609c334ce39ff3e0446f395c07e299.

4   Chas Smith, "Devastating Rumor Proves True as World Surf League Vindictively Cancels Bethany Hamilton over Trans-Exclusionary Views!," BeachGrit, March 1, 2023, https://beachgrit.com/2023/03/devastating-rumor-proves-true-as-world-surf-league-vindictively-cancels-bethany-hamilton-over-trans-exclusionary-views/.

5   Chas Smith, "Confirmed: World Surf League Brass Informed Championship Tour Surfer He Was Not Allowed to Celebrate Bethany Hamilton on International Women's Day!," BeachGrit, March 15, 2023, https://beachgrit.com/2023/03/confirmed-world-surf-league-brass-informed-championship-tour-surfer-he-was-not-allowed-to-celebrate-bethany-hamilton-on-international-womens-day/.

6   Postmedia Sports, "High School Trans Athlete Wins High-Jumping Event, Sparking Outrage . . .," Toronto Sun, February 14, 2024, https://torontosun.com/sports/other-sports/high-school-trans-athlete-wins-high-jumping-event-sparking-outrage.

7   Ibid.

8   Jacquelyn Palumbo, "Miss Netherlands Pageant Crowns First Trans Winner, Rikkie Valerie Kollé," CNN, July 10, 2023, https://www.cnn.com/style/miss-netherlands-pageant-rikkie-kolle/index.html.

9   Andrew Chapados, "'misgendering' Would Be a Crime with a Possible 2-Year Jail Sentence under the UK's Far-Left Labour Party," Blaze Media, October 17, 2023, https://www.theblaze.com/news/uk-labour-party-misgendering-crime.

10   "The Fourteenth Amendment and the Evolution of Title IX," United States Courts, https://www.uscourts.gov/educational-resources/educational-activities/14th-amendment-and-evolution-title-ix#:~:text=Specifically%2C%20Title%20IX%20states%20that,activity%20receiving%20Federal%20financial%20assistance.%E2%80%9D

11 R. Shep Melnick, The Transformation of Title IX: Regulating Gender Equality in Education (Washington, D.C.: The Brookings Institution, 2018), 4.

12 Chirag Radhyan, "'if Mike Tyson Identifies as a Female, Should He Be Allowed to Enter a Boxing Match with a Biological Female?': Jon Jones, Usain Bolt, and Sporting World Likes US Representative's Burning Question amid Trans Athletes and Locker Room Saga," *EssentiallySports*, June 8, 2023, https://www.essentiallysports.com /boxing-news-if-mike-tyson-identifies-as-a-female-should-he-be-allowed -to-enter-a-boxing-match-with-a-biological-female-jon-jones-usain-bolt -and-sporting-world-likes-us-representatives-burning-question/.

13 Caroline Downey, "Judge Jackson Refuses to Define 'Woman' during Confirmation Hearing: 'I'm Not a Biologist,'" *National Review*, March 23, 2022, https://www.nationalreview.com/news/judge-jackson-refuses -to-define-woman-during-confirmation-hearing-im-not-a-biologist/.

14 Jessica Chasmar, "Woke Liberals Push to Replace 'Mother' with 'Birthing Parent' to Appease Transgender Community," Fox News, July 7, 2022, https://www.foxnews.com/politics/woke-liberals-push-replace -mother-birthing-parent-appease-transgender.

15 *Budget of the U.S. Government* (Washington, D.C.: Office of Management and Budget, 2022), 18.

16 Keith Griffith, "I Know He's Not Familiar with a Woman's Body': AOC's Bizarre Insult to 40-Years-Married Greg Abbott over New Texas Abortion Law and Says 'Six Weeks Pregnant Means Two Weeks Late for Period,'" *Daily Mail*, September 7, 20202, https://www.dailymail.co.uk /news/article-9967997/AOC-calls-women-menstruating-people-blasting -Texas-Governor-abortion-law.html.

17 Madeleine Kearns, "Women and Mothers Aren't 'Chestfeeders,'" *National Review*, February 11, 2021, https://www.nationalreview.com /corner/women-and-mothers-arent-chestfeeders/.

18 "Watch: Far-Left Berkeley Law Professor Melts Down When Senator Hawley Asks Her If Men Can Get Pregnant," Hawley Senate website, July 12, 2022, https://www.hawley.senate.gov/watch-far-left-berkeley -law-professor-melts-down-when-senator-hawley-asks-her-if-men-can -get.

19 Ibid.

20   Tyler Clifford, "Biden Administration Proposes Title IX Protections for Transgender Students," Reuters, June 23, 2022, https://www.reuters.com /world/us/biden-administration-proposes-title-ix-protections -transgender-students-2022–06-23/.

Chapter 8

1   "New Poll: School Choice Support Soars from 2020," American Federation for Children, July 11, 2023, https://www.federationforchildren .org/new-poll-school-choice-support-soars-from-2020/.

2   Joshua Q. Nelson and Fox News, "Teachers Union Boss Randi Weingarten Claims School Choice 'Undermines Democracy,'" Fox News, December 20, 2023, https://www.foxnews.com/media/teacher-union -boss-randi-weingarten-claims-school-choice-undermines-democracy.

3   Sara Chernikoff, "1 in 5 Americans Have Low-Literacy Skills: These Charts Explain Reading Levels in the US," *USA Today*, September 9, 2023, https://www.usatoday.com/story/news/education/2023/09/09 /literacy-levels-in-the-us/70799429007/.

4   Alvin Parker and Alvin ParkerHey, "US Literacy Rate Statistics for 2024 (Trends & Data)," Prosperity For All, December 26, 2023, https://www .prosperityforamerica.org/literacy-statistics/.

5   Joshua Q. Nelson and Fox News, "Teachers Union Boss Defends Sending Son to Private School after Calling School Choice Racist," Fox News, September 14, 2023, https://www.foxnews.com/media /teachers-union-boss-defends-sending-son-private-school.

6   Jim Newell, "McAuliffe Lost Because He's a Democrat," Slate Magazine, November 3, 2021, https://slate.com/news-and-politics/2021/11/terry -mcauliffe-glenn-youngkin-virginia-democrats.html.

7   Ibid.

8   Names have been changed to protect the student's privacy.

9   Abigail Shrier, "How a Dad Lost Custody of Son after Questioning His Transgender Identity," *New York Post*, February 26, 2022, https://nypost.com/2022/02/26/dad-lost-custody-after-questioning-sons -transgender-identity/.

10   "Family Services Policy Manual," Department for Children and Families, accessed February 16, 2024, https://dcf.vermont.gov/fsd/policies.

11   Jeff Johnston, "Boston Children's Hospital under Fire for 'Transgender' Interventions That Damage and Disfigure Children," *Daily Citizen*,

August 19, 2022, https://dailycitizen.focusonthefamily.com/boston
-childrens-hospital-under-fire-for-transgender-interventions-that
-damage-and-disfigure-children/.

12   Libs of Tik Tok, "Boston Children's Hospital Says That Toddlers Can
Know They Are Transgender. Some Signs Are Refusing a Haircut or
Playing with the Opposite Gender Toys," Facebook post, August 14,
2022, https://www.facebook.com/watch/?v=842459790073958.

13   "Treatment of Gender Dysphoria for Children and Adolescents," Florida
Department of Health, April 20, 2022, https://content.govdelivery.com
/accounts/FLDOH/bulletins/3143d4c.

14   (@BillboardChris), "'A good portion of children do know . . . ,'" Twitter,
August 14, 2022, 10:30 a.m., https://twitter.com/BillboardChris
/status/1558823459651817477.

15   Ibid.

16   (@BillboardChris), "Boston Children's Hospital has hidden . . . ,"
Twitter, August 11, 2022, 12:58 p.m., https://twitter.com/BillboardChris
/status/1557773583618908161.

17   Kristen Monaco, "Gender-Affirming Chest Surgeries Increase by
Nearly 5x in Teens," *MedPage Today*, October 17, 2022, https://www
.medpagetoday.com/pediatrics/generalpediatrics/101252.

18   Ryan Chatelain, "Study Estimates Trans Youth Population Has Doubled
in 5 Years," Spectrum News NY1, June 10, 2022, https://www.ny1.com
/nyc/all-boroughs/news/2022/06/10/study-estimates-transgender-youth
-population-has-doubled-in-5-years.

19   Craig Monger, "FDA Adds New Warning for Commonly Used Puberty
Blockers," *1819 News*, August 6, 2022, https://1819news.com/news/item
/fda-adds-new-warning-to-commonly-used-puberty-blockers.

20   Tulsi Gabbard, "80% of transgender people who seek . . . ," TikTok,
November 17, 2022, https://www.tiktok.com/@tulsigabbard
/video/7166937827278589230.

21   Ryan Chatelain, "Study Estimates Transgender Youth Population
Has Doubled in 5 Years," Spectrum News NY1, June 10,
2022, https://ny1.com/nyc/all-boroughs/news/2022/06/10/study
-estimates-transgender-youth-population-has-doubled-in-5-years.

22   Carolyn Crist, "Nearly Half of Companies Say They Plan to Eliminate
Bachelor's Degree Requirements in 2024," HR Dive, December 12,

2023, https://www.hrdive.com/news/nearly-half-of-companies-plan -to-eliminate-bachelors-degree-requirements/702235/#:~:text=In%20 2023%2C%2055%25%20of%20companies,other%20ways%20to%20 gain%20skills.

23   Carolyn Crist, "Nearly Half of Companies Say They Plan to Eliminate Bachelor's Degree Requirements in 2024," *HR Dive*, December 12, 2023, https://www.hrdive.com/news/nearly-half-of-companies-plan -to-eliminate-bachelors-degree-requirements/702235/#:~:text=In%20 2023%2C%2055%25%20of%20companies,other%20ways%20to%20 gain%20skills.